THE PSYCHOLOGY CAREERS COMPASS

This book offers a practical and accessible guide to support anyone who wants to pursue a career in psychology and work in mental health and associated areas.

Based on UK applied psychologist career paths, featuring psychologist profiles from across the main disciplines, this book illuminates the possibilities of a career in psychology. It outlines the varied and exciting different applied areas to consider, including clinical, educational, forensic, counselling, health, occupational, sports and exercise psychology, and academic and research careers. This book provides career guidance for each area of applied psychology, along with case studies that offer real-life examples from practitioners in the field, including those from racially minoritised groups. The author discusses each area, what different psychologists do, qualifications and experience needed, and different routes, presenting all the information necessary to make informed decisions about a career in psychology.

Offering an inclusive, realistic and clear overview of what it's like to build and maintain a career in the applied psychology professions, this book is for all students, graduates and career transitioners looking to understand their career options in the field.

Grace Mansah-Owusu is an organisational psychologist and runs her own career development and training consultancy in the UK called Great Minds for Business. Along with a career spanning over 15 years in work and organisational psychology and experience in various industries, including transport, logistics, hospitality, charity and not-for-profit, and consultancy, she has an MSc in occupational psychology and a PhD in career development. Grace is passionate about supporting people in their careers and providing timely and accurate support to anyone at any career stage.

THE PSYCHOLOGY CAREERS COMPASS

Applied Psychology Career Pathways for All

Grace Mansah-Owusu

Routledge
Taylor & Francis Group
LONDON AND NEW YORK

Designed cover image: Getty Images

First published 2027
by Routledge
4 Park Square, Milton Park, Abingdon, Oxon OX14 4RN

and by Routledge
605 Third Avenue, New York, NY 10158

Routledge is an imprint of the Taylor & Francis Group, an informa business

British Library Cataloguing-in-Publication Data
A catalogue record for this book is available from the British Library

Library of Congress Cataloging-in-Publication Data
Names: Mansah-Owusu, Grace author
Title: The psychology careers compass: applied psychology career pathways for all / Grace Mansah-Owusu.
Description: Abingdon, Oxon; New York, NY: Routledge, 2027. | Includes bibliographical references and index.
Identifiers: LCCN 2026023227 (print) | LCCN 2026023228 (ebook) | ISBN 9781041133698 hardback | ISBN 9781041131601 paperback | ISBN 9781003669449 ebook
Subjects: LCSH: Psychology—Vocational guidance
Classification: LCC BF76 .M3155 2027 (print) | LCC BF76 (ebook)
LC record available at https://lccn.loc.gov/2026023227
LC ebook record available at https://lccn.loc.gov/2026023228

ISBN: 978-1-041-13369-8 (hbk)
ISBN: 978-1-041-13160-1 (pbk)
ISBN: 978-1-003-66944-9 (ebk)

DOI: 10.4324/9781003669449

Typeset in Sabon
by codeMantra

CONTENTS

FIGURES

TABLES

INTRODUCTION

WHY DO PEOPLE CHOOSE TO STUDY PSYCHOLOGY?

This book is called *The Psychology Careers Compass: Applied Psychology Career Pathways for All* for many reasons. When people think of careers in psychology, a stereotypical image may come to mind that includes "The clinical psychologist, images of a white coat-clad professional with glasses and a notebook, listening to patients' worries."

Undergraduate or postgraduate students may enter the field of psychology for various reasons. Here are a few reasons that may resonate with you.

1. Understand oneself and others – one motivation for studying this subject is to understand how people think and develop. Understanding motivations and psychological and physiological drivers and motivators is a core foundation of a psychology course. Some people may be drawn to the area due to having mental health challenges themselves or having a friend or a family member with mental illness.

DOI: 10.4324/9781003669449-1

2. Have a positive impact on others – some people are driven to study the subject as they want to support, help or assist others.
3. Give something back to the community – another driver to pursue a career within a psychological field is to give back to society and provide psychological support to those who need it, either in the general population or those in mental health or psychological support services.
4. Some are drawn to this career area as they are interested in the topic and have no real plans to pursue a career in the area.

HOW TO USE THIS BOOK

This book is intended to serve as a guide for anyone interested in careers within the psychological field, and it is written from a UK perspective. Pathways, qualifications and experience levels required to qualify in other countries outside the UK may differ significantly. If you are based outside the UK, I encourage you to supplement the information in this book with more locally focused resources.

APPLIED PSYCHOLOGY

The term applied psychology is defined as the use of psychological methods to solve practical problems related to human and animal behaviour. The various aspects of applied psychology can range from laboratory studies to clinical observations, to supporting athletes in achieving peak performance, to developing learning interventions for individuals with neurodivergent conditions.[1]

Widely speaking, applied psychology includes specialisms such as developmental, clinical, counselling, educational, forensic, health, neuro, occupational and sports and exercise psychology. The list below provides an overview of each area.

- **Developmental psychology** – developmental psychologists are interested in all aspects of human development from a person's infancy to old age. These psychologists aim to understand patterns of development and consider how these factors may differ across ages, regions and other environmental factors. Developmental psychologists often work within the field of educational psychology.

- **Clinical psychology** – This area aims to reduce distress and encourage psychological wellbeing for individuals. Clinical psychologists are responsible for the assessment and treatment of conditions such as depression, anxiety and use interventions such as cognitive behavioural therapy in different populations, including children, the elderly and adult populations. Clinical psychologists can work within the National Health Service (NHS) or in private practice.
- **Counselling psychology** – Counselling psychologists focus on working with people facing different psychological and mental health challenges. Counselling psychologists also create tailored psychological support to increase wellbeing. Counselling psychologists can work within the NHS, privately or within charities or other institutions.
- **Educational psychology** – Educational psychologists support people (often children and young people) who may experience difficulties in educational and learning institutions such as schools and further education colleges. Mostly, educational psychologists work within local authorities to support people within those areas. Educational psychologists work with other professionals, including teachers and other educational specialists, to create inclusive learning environments.
- **Forensic psychology** – forensic psychologists specialise in applying psychology to criminal behaviour. Forensic psychologists can work within the criminal justice system and often perform a combination of tasks, including providing assessments of the mental health of individuals involved in legal proceedings. They can also research criminal behaviour and provide treatment programmes for those with mental health conditions who have committed crimes. Forensic psychologists often work within prisons and institutions for young offenders.

- **Health psychology** – This specialism is concerned with promoting and maintaining wellbeing and healthy behaviours. Health psychologists are trained to understand both the emotional and psychological aspects of health and illness and can bring improvements in health and other behaviours. Health psychologists can work within local councils, charities, universities and other organisations concerned with monitoring the health of individuals such as the NHS.
- **Neuropsychology** – this area of psychology is concerned with the relationship and link between behaviour and the brain. Neuropsychologists focus on specific brain injuries and how these conditions may affect cognitive and emotional functions of the body and mind. Neuropsychologists diagnose and develop rehabilitation methods for people with neurological conditions, brain injuries and neurodevelopmental conditions. Mostly, neuropsychologists work within the NHS research institutes and universities.
- **Occupational psychology** – this area of psychology is concerned with applying psychological principles to the workplace and organisations. Occupational psychologists are also called industrial, work, business or organisational psychologists and they work to create optimal working environments for employees and organisations. Occupational psychologists help organisations understand people and offer evidence-based solutions to improve employee satisfaction, training and work processes. They are concerned with creating psychometric assessments for the selection and evaluation of candidates in job processes, coaching and guiding individuals in their careers and designing workplace wellbeing strategies. Occupational psychologists can work within the private sector, public sector and non-profit organisations.
- **Sports and exercise psychology** – This area of psychology focuses on applying psychological principles to enhance sport, exercise and athletic performance. Sports and exercise psychologists are also concerned with promoting wellbeing in athletes and the public. Sports and exercise psychologists work to improve motivation, self-belief and help people

overcome mental and emotional challenges related to sports or exercise. Sports psychologists can work with coaches, referees and athletes; they can also work with the public to encourage exercise and participation in sport.

These areas of applied psychology offer different routes into the field of psychology. If you would like to understand these areas further, this book is for you.

Origins of psychology: a historical context

Some people think that psychology, and the study of it, is something new to the human condition. However, for centuries, individuals have been fascinated and preoccupied with how people think, feel and do things and this is the case across cultures and nations.

Psychology is the study of the human mind and has its origins in countries and cultures including Egypt, Persia, Greece, China and India. Researchers from Germany are often credited with creating the first experimental designs, such as Gustav Fechner in 1854, who researched how sensory experiences are made and how to experiment on them. Subsequently, Wilhelm Wundt founded the first psychological laboratory in Germany in 1879 and self-identified as a psychologist. These were in the 19th century. These began an explosion of investigation into psychological theories to explain the human condition. This also led to the specialist and applied areas of psychological study, such as humanistic, behavioural and cognitive psychology as well as processes such as psychoanalysis. Researchers began to be intrigued and interested in learning and how people acquire information.

This gave rise to theories such as operant and classical conditioning from B.F. Skinner and Ivan Pavlov and their famous experiments have shaped a lot about how we think about people and learning. Psychology was popularised during the 19th and 20th centuries and has definitely become increasingly popular as a treatment method for mental and psychological distress and as a profession and career path.

Diversity in psychology: a UK perspective

As someone who has been in and around the field of psychology for over 20 years, I have observed how the profession has changed and evolved. The following section highlights some of the governing and professional bodies that centre around psychology and psychological careers, and they often publish data and research that highlight different areas of diversity within professional psychologists. These statistics illustrate the diversity of the profession.

ETHNICITY

According to a Health Care Professionals Council (HCPC) survey from 2020,[2] 90% of registered practitioner psychologists identified as white, 4.3% Asian, 1.7% Black and 3.6% identified as other.

GENDER

According to the 2020 HCPC paper, female practitioner psychologists accounted for the most psychology practitioners in the UK (75.4%), males account for 23.5%, and those who identify as other genders account for 1.1%.

SEXUAL ORIENTATION

7% of UK registered practitioner psychologists identified as Gay, Lesbian or Queer and 88% identified as heterosexual and 5% identified as other (HCPC, 2020).

DISABILITY

21% of the UK population have identified as disabled, while 12% of practitioner psychologists identify as having a disability, according to the HCPC research. 5.2% of junior academics and 3.7% of senior academics identified as having a disability.

This data paints a picture that, despite some areas of psychology being diverse (e.g., gender), this diversity is not well represented at senior levels of psychological professions, and most of the profession is not representative of the UK population, even regarding Census data. In other dimensions of diversity, such as ethnicity and disability, it is evident that the psychology professions in the UK need to be more representative. The psychology profession also needs to create organisational environments that foster and support inclusion. These workplace environments shouldn't only be recruiting more diverse staff to create a stronger, more relatable set of psychological practitioners; these staff should also feel included and like they belong in these organisations and not excluded or prevented from progressing within them.

DIVERSITY INITIATIVES IN PSYCHOLOGICAL PROFESSIONS

According to a paper by Kancelijak and Calia (2023),[3] the profession is heavily influenced by white, male heteronormative and able-bodied individuals. Notably, some areas of psychology, particularly those related to frontline healthcare, such as clinical psychology and child and adolescent psychology, have initiatives to address health inequalities in mental health and to improve access to psychological services and training. Health Education England (HEE)[4] has implemented a mentoring scheme to support aspiring ethnic minority leaders across mental health training programmes.

For clinical psychology, HEE developed a mental health implementation plan for the NHS in England, setting a target to recruit over 2,500 practitioner psychologists by 2023/2024. This led to a 60% expansion in entry for NHS-funded places on the Doctorate in Clinical Psychology for 2020 and 2021. The aims of the HEE implementation plan were to:

- To improve access for clinical psychologists into the profession. An action plan was developed to improve equity of access and inclusion for people from racially minoritised groups who wanted to access clinical psychology training.
- Additionally, HEE provided funding to all the clinical psychology training universities to provide mentoring schemes for racially minoritised groups to apply for clinical psychology training.

- Lastly, HEE commissioned NHS Trusts to deliver paid experience schemes and offer opportunities to those from lower socioeconomic backgrounds and aspire to gain experience in the field.

HOW CAN PSYCHOLOGY BECOME MORE REPRESENTATIVE?

Some of these initiatives are good; however, the nature of the different applied areas of psychology means that the processes, qualifications and career paths vary quite widely. Based on this, there are quite big differences in access to the profession and inclusion in different areas. Additionally, these initiatives need to be evaluated to see if they fulfil the original aims.

Some ideas that can help improve the inclusion and diversity of the profession include:

1. In each applied area, e.g., clinical, counselling, educational etc., ensure there is an active action plan to monitor diversity and inclusion and structured initiatives. Have frequent monitoring and evaluations of these initiatives.
2. Active outreach, universities and workplaces. Workforces should play a more structured and active role in schools, colleges and universities to ensure that those interested are better aware of psychological professions.
3. Improve access to psychological professions in these specific groups based on the HCPC data on diversity of registered psychologists, e.g., people with disabilities, women at senior levels of psychology, including research publishers, people from racially minoritised groups and monitor initiatives at least every two years.

Qualification routes in psychology (UK)

So, you have decided to pursue a career in psychology, or you want to understand more about what you may experience if you pursue this career path. This section will identify what you need to learn and obtain at school and university to qualify as a psychologist.

WHAT DO I NEED TO KNOW IF I AM IN HIGH SCHOOL/SECONDARY SCHOOL?

If you are completing your General Certificate of Secondary Education (GCSE), you will need good grades in the core subjects: English, Maths and Science if you want to pursue a career in psychology. You may be thinking, what is a good grade at this level? The general guidelines highlight that most universities will require you to have a grade 4/C in GCSEs, including English, Maths and Science, as well as other additional subjects that you may be doing.

After your GCSEs, you are likely to go on to further education after the age of 16.

If you are completing A-levels and want to apply to an undergraduate psychology degree, you will often be expected to have studied at least one numerical subject and this includes (chemistry, physics, maths, geography, economics, statistics, computing, biology or psychology).

If you are completing a Business and Technology Education Council (BTEC) qualification, you are likely to be accepted onto most psychology degrees at different universities. However, it is best to check each institution's specific eligibility criteria. You will mostly need at Distinction, Distinction, Merit-Distinction, Distinction, Distinction (DDM-DDD) in a science-based subject or a Merit, Merit, Merit (MMM) grade to be accepted onto a psychology undergraduate degree. If you are completing an International Baccalaureate, you will need a 6, 6, 6, at Higher Level. Some universities may require a 6 in Higher Level Maths, a science subject or both.

Undergraduate degree types

Applying for psychology undergraduate degrees can feel overwhelming. When choosing an undergraduate degree from a UK

Table 0.1 Table regarding the difference between a BA and BSc degree

Psychology undergraduate course Bachelor of Arts (BA)	*Psychology undergraduate course Bachelor of Science (BSc)*
Focus on social and behavioural aspects of psychology and may include optional modules outside of psychology e.g., in humanities or other social sciences	May focus more on the scientific and mathematical parts of psychology and offer modules including: neuropsychology, psychopharmacology, biological basis in psychology
Research methods: may place more emphasis on qualitative research methods such as interviews or focus groups	Research methods: may place more emphasis on quantitative research methods including questionnaires, lab studies including MRI scanning for example

university, there are some key things to consider. One of the main decisions you will need to make is whether to pursue a Bachelor of Arts (BA) or a Bachelor of Science (BSc). Broadly speaking, a BA degree typically focuses more on the social aspects of psychology. In contrast, a BSc will focus more on numerical and biological areas of psychology, including quantitative research methods, statistics and biological psychology (Table 0.1).

When you are choosing an undergraduate degree, one of the most important things you need to know and understand is how you learn best. For example, if you lean more heavily on arts and prefer a less scientific approach, maybe look for a BA degree in psychology; in comparison, if you like more numerical reasoning and scientific research and enquiry, look for a BSc degree in psychology.

Undergraduate degrees provide a solid foundation for pursuing a career in psychology. They provide skills in critical thinking, data analysis, written and verbal communication, teamwork, organisational skills, planning and scientific rigour. These skills can be valuable across a wide range of professions, not only in psychological ones.

The BPS accredits specific undergraduate degree courses in the UK. The BPS does this to ensure that courses meet minimum standards for teaching and learning in psychology careers. This is the biggest stamp of approval if you want to pursue further study in psychology after your first degree. Neither a BA nor a BSc is better; it's what suits you and your learning style best.

British Psychological Society degree accreditation

The BPS is the professional body for psychologists in the UK and the BPS accredits undergraduate and postgraduate psychological degrees. This means that accredited courses must include specific modules and assess knowledge in particular ways to ensure that standards and requirements are met. If you complete an accredited course, you will gain what is called the Graduate Basis for Chartered Membership (GBC) and this is a crucial step to pursue further study within the psychology profession. Both BA and BSc courses are accredited by the BPS and if you would like to see which courses they are, you can have a look on the BPS website.[5]

Additionally, if you started your degree from 2006 onwards and obtained a third-class degree classification (40% average grade across all modules), you won't be eligible for Graduate Basis for Chartered Membership and would need to complete a psychology conversion course to go on to further study in psychology and be a chartered member.

Undergraduate degrees with foundation years

Another option to consider when applying for an undergraduate degree at university is an integrated four-year degree, which includes a foundation year. If you cannot or do not end up being accepted onto a traditional psychology degree programme, a foundation degree integrated into a BA or BSc programme can open doors.

The foundation degree provides an alternative entry route to university for students who may not meet the traditional entry requirements for a three- or four-year degree. The foundation year enables learners to develop academic skills and build knowledge before beginning a main degree. This may be due to not achieving the required grades to enter a traditional degree course. To find these integrated degrees, you can check the BPS website and verify if the degree you are interested in has Graduate Basis for Chartered Membership (GBC). You can also check through Universities and Colleges Admissions Service (UCAS) to find foundation year integrated degrees.

What undergraduate degree grade do I need to get onto a postgraduate course or a doctorate programme?

Degree grades for UK undergraduate degrees are graded in this way (Table 0.2).

Typically, most people are accepted onto master's courses with a 2:1 or a first-class degree at undergraduate level. However, you can gain admission to a master's course with a 2:2, but it might be slightly harder. Gaining some work experience, paid and or voluntary may help you get onto a master's degree course with a 2:2 grade and may help support your application.

IS IT NECESSARY FOR ME TO DO A MASTER'S DEGREE FOR A PROFESSIONAL CAREER IN PSYCHOLOGY?

In the subsequent chapters, which discuss each applied area of psychology, we will address this question more thoroughly.

Table 0.2 Undergraduate degree classifications

Grade	*Percentage*
First-class (first)	70%+
2.1 (upper second class)	60%–69%
2.2 (lower second class)	50%–59%
Third-class	40%–49%
Fail	0%–40%

The short answer is that it depends on which area of psychology you want to go into, or if you already have an undergraduate degree in psychology, or plan to get one.

For some areas of psychology, including health, occupational, counselling, forensic and sports and exercise psychology, the master's degree counts as the stage two part of the final professional qualification required to become a chartered psychologist. For other areas of psychology, including, Clinical and Educational Psychology, a master's is not a prerequisite, and you can complete a professional doctorate without one.

However, an increasing number of people are opting to pursue master's degrees in these fields out of interest and to stand out when applying to doctoral programmes. As noted previously, master's degrees in clinical and educational psychology are not required.

Psychology conversion degrees

Psychology conversion master's degrees are postgraduate degrees for people who hold an undergraduate degree in different subject other than psychology and wish to pursue a career in the field. Psychology conversion degrees are also for those who hold an unaccredited psychology degree and aim to become professional chartered psychologists. For example, this includes psychology degrees without BPS accreditation, such as those started after 2006 and awarded a third-class degree classification, as well as joint honours degrees or psychology degrees from different countries. Psychology conversion master's degrees provide learners with the knowledge and methods necessary to meet the academic rigour and expertise required in a career in psychology. Additionally, these courses provide the holder with the Graduate Basis for Chartered Membership (GBC), which is required to become a chartered applied psychologist.

Psychology conversion courses teach the core areas, including biological, cognitive and social psychology. The main purpose of these degrees is to prepare people for a career in the profession. The information learned on a conversion course is the same as what is covered in a traditional three-year undergraduate degree; the difference is that you get less time. The courses last either one year full-time or two years part-time.

Here are some modules you may find on a psychology conversion master's degree:

- Introduction to psychology
- Cognitive psychology
- Research methods
- Social psychology
- Developmental psychology
- Biological psychology
- Individual differences
- Research project

Psychology conversion master's degree courses range from about £11,000 to £13,000 for a one-year course for home students and can be much higher for international students, e.g., from £18,000 to over £30,00 for the year.

CASE STUDY

Chinwe Anyaorah, clinical psychologist

Chinwe Anyaorah is a trainee clinical psychologist at UCL who completed a psychology conversion master's degree at Queen's University Belfast after completing an undergraduate degree in Japanese and Economics. Chinwe speaks about her experience on the conversation course here:

> Honestly, I found the conversion course pretty comprehensive. We covered a lot of core topics over the year. That said, sometimes it felt like we didn't go into much depth, probably because there just wasn't enough time. This might be university specific, but I was given a lot of support to do a completely original thesis that allowed me to gain a lot of helpful research skills. The course was BPS-accredited, so the content was quite structured.

Knowledge wise, I don't think I was too far behind others had done a full psychology undergraduate degree and then a more specialist master's. But I did feel a bit behind more in terms of confidence and seeing myself as someone who belonged in psychology. When I started the conversion course, I had no idea what I wanted to do, I actually didn't even know what clinical psychology was! It was during the course that I discovered it as a possible path. Even then, when I mentioned it to the careers advisor, her response wasn't very encouraging. She emphasised how competitive it was and actually tried to steer me toward occupational psychology instead, funnily enough.

Funding your studies – 'It's all about the money'

Money makes the world go round and it also pays for things, including study. You may be wondering, how much is this career going to cost me?

Funding undergraduate study

If you are an English Home student, this means you are eligible for a student loan and can borrow money to help pay for tuition fees and living costs. You may be able to borrow more if you come from a low-income home, you are disabled or you have children. You may also be eligible even if you are not from the UK.[6] The terms of the loans are such that you only start paying back when you earn over a certain amount and your repayments depend on what you earn after you reach that threshold.

Your eligibility for student finance depends on these things:

1. The university or college you are applying for.
2. The course you are applying for or the course you are on.
3. If you have completed a higher education course before.
4. Your age.
5. Nationality and/or residency status.

Both BA and BSc courses are eligible for funding through the student loan, as well as the foundation years. This is also the case if you are studying full-time or part-time. There's no upper age limit for tuition fee loans or grants.

YOUR NATIONALITY AND RESIDENCY STATUS

If you have UK citizenship and you are based in England and you have lived in the UK, the Channel Islands or the Isle of Man for three years before the first day of your first academic year, you are eligible for a student loan.

IF YOU HAVE A DIFFERENT NATIONALITY OR YOU LIVE OUTSIDE THE UK AND YOU ARE A UK CITIZEN

Using the undergraduate student finance checker on the gov.uk website[7] can help you understand if you are eligible for student loan support. Student loans through the English government are one way to fund undergraduate study. However, there are scholarships, bursaries and grants you can apply for to support yourself financially. These additional sources of funding don't have to be repaid.

Scholarships

Students who may be more likely to gain a scholarship include those students who are:

1. From low-income backgrounds.
2. From underrepresented backgrounds, e.g., ethnicity, gender, first in your family to go to university, live in an area where lower levels of people go to university, mature students.
3. Disabled students.
4. Students who have experience being in care.
5. Those who have a placement year attached to their undergraduate course.

6. Those who have performed and are seen as academically outstanding.
7. Some non-UK students.

    1. The university you are accepted to, when you are applying for your student loan will calculate your household income and often will provide you with the shortfall in the form of a loan. Usually, low income, depending on the university you are applying to, can be anything from £16,000 to £60,000.
    2. People from underrepresented groups include first-generation university students, those from underrepresented ethnic groups, those living in areas with low university attendance, and mature students. People who fall into these groups can access widening participation funding at their chosen university. Eligibility varies per university, so it's worth checking. When assessing an individual's status, things that may be looked at include: your postcode, your school, your household income, if you are a young carer or you have been in care.
    3. Students who are applying to university and have a disability can receive a Disabled Students Allowance (DSA). Other funding sources include an organisation called the Snowdon Trust, who offer grants to help people with disabilities in higher or further education to meet additional costs that may not be covered.

        - The Student Health Association also offers a bursary that enables students with disabilities to continue their studies.
        - England and Wales: students who have been in care, if you have been in local authority care, (e.g., not looked after by your parents) you may be entitled to a higher education bursary of at least £2,000 if you start higher education before your 25th birthday, contact your local authority for details.
        - Scotland: those who have been in care are eligible for a £9,000 care-experienced student bursary that

you don't repay and an optional student loan of up to £2,400.

- Northern Ireland: Your Trust will assist with your application for funding for higher education.

  Other organisations that can assist you which offer grants, bursaries and scholarships include:

- The Unite Foundation, who offer accommodation and bills covered for up to three years whilst you are at university, if you attend some of the organisation's partner universities.
- Buttle UK is a charity aiming to help children and young people who have experienced crisis, dealing with multiple challenging social issues or financial hardship.

4. Academic merit scholarships.

   These scholarships depend on the grades you get before you go to university. Contact your university to enquire about available academic scholarships.[8]

Funding postgraduate studies

This section may be somewhat complex, as funding options vary across both education levels. However, the main message is that there are funding options available at each level, either via loans, scholarships or grants.

FUNDING FOR MASTER'S DEGREES

If you are pursuing a career in forensic, occupational, sports or exercise psychology, or neuropsychology, you are likely to complete a master's degree, as it's part of the qualification route. For these stages, funding may be something that you are worried and/or concerned about.

If you are a UK resident living in England and studying a taught or research master's course in the UK, you may be eligible for an English postgraduate student loan. This loan allows you to borrow up to £12,471 towards your tuition fees, study and living expenses (for the year commencing 2024/2025). This loan from student finance is not means-tested so it doesn't depend on your household income, so you can choose how much you want to borrow.

Eligibility is based on being:

- A UK national or have settled status.
- Normally live in England.
- Have lived in the UK, the Channel Islands or the Isle of Man for the past three years.
- Be under age 60 on the first day of the first academic year of your course.
- Not already have a master's degree or higher qualification.

POSTGRADUATE LOAN REPAYMENT

You start repaying the loan in April, after your course finishes, at a rate of 6% on any amount over £21,000, or £1,750 per month before tax. As with undergraduate student loans, deductions are made directly from your salary.

SCHOLARSHIPS AND BURSARIES

Scholarships

If you are an international student wanting to complete a master's degree in the UK, the British Council offers GREAT scholarships for those who are from a variety of different countries, including Bangladesh, China, Egypt, France, Ghana, Greece, India, Indonesia, Italy, Kenya, Malaysia, Mexico, Nigeria, Pakistan, Spain, Thailand, Turkey and Vietnam. You can find out more about them at study-uk.britishcouncil.org/scholarships-funding/great-scholarships.

CHEVENING SCHOLARSHIPS

These scholarships are funded by the Foreign, Commonwealth and Development Office and partner organisations and are awarded to international students who have demonstrable leadership potential and strong academic backgrounds. They offer full financial support to study any master's degree at any UK university. The scholarship covers tuition fees, living expenses and return flights to the UK. Scholars need to have ambition, leadership potential and a clear plan for making a positive impact in their communities.

COMMONWEALTH SCHOLARSHIPS

These are awarded to people with the potential to make a positive impact on the global stage and every year around 700 students are chosen to be Commonwealth scholars at UK universities. The scholarship is for those who may not otherwise be able to afford UK study without this scholarship and the scheme is for future leaders and innovators. You will need to have an undergraduate degree at 2:1 grade or above.

The financial support covers tuition fees, airfare to and from the UK and a living allowance when you are here. You can apply for this qualification through a National Nominating Agency, a university or a non-governmental organisation. You can find out more about it via the British Council.[9]

Additionally, alumni discounts are available at different universities. This means if you have studied a course at a university before (e.g., undergraduate), you may be eligible for a discount to complete your next course. Each university's rules differ, but it may be a way to reduce your expenses.

UNIVERSITY SPECIFIC BURSARIES

For additional information on bursaries, please have a look at each university you are applying for and check what's available for home and international students.

Funding doctoral degrees

Research councils

These options are primarily for people completing a PhD research doctorate, rather than a professional doctorate, which is offered to complete a person's training in any psychological field. You can also self-fund these professional doctorates and in counselling, forensic, occupational, sports, exercise and health psychology.

Research councils connect with universities and provide funding to Doctoral Training Partnerships or Centres for Doctoral Training. There are seven research councils in the UK, and research councils provide studentships which include fees and a 'stipend' (a wage) which is paid tax-free. These research councils primarily fund PhDs or research doctoral degrees. These funding opportunities aren't available for professional doctorates e.g., any professional doctorates to qualify as a professional psychologist (this difference will be explained in the next section). The most likely research council-related to psychological research is the Economic and Social Research Council. These funds support PhD research degrees.

Other organisations that fund doctoral research PhDs include universities themselves as well as commercial and charitable organisations such as The Wellcome Trust, Cancer Research UK, The Leverhulme Trust and many more.

SELF-FUNDING THROUGH LOANS OR WORK

If you are unable to secure funding for your doctoral degrees through studentships or other ways, you can try self-funding, i.e. paying your own way through your studies. You can use doctoral degree funding from the Student Loans Company, or consider a few bank loans available, such as professional or career development loans. You can also work as a research assistant.

DOCTORAL STUDY LOANS

- The postgraduate doctoral loan can help with fees and living costs whilst studying a doctoral course. This loan is the postgraduate version of the undergraduate student loan.
- To be eligible for a student loan to fund doctoral studies, you can be studying full or part-time, taught or research-based or both.
- You must be 60 on the first day of your course or on the first day of the first academic year.

- You need to be a UK or Irish citizen or have settled status under the EU Settlement Scheme or indefinite leave to remain.
- You live in England.
- You have lived in the UK, the Channel Islands or the Isle of Man for three years in a row.
- You may also be eligible if you are a refugee, you have settled status.
- If you are 18 and over and have lived in the UK for at least half of your life or at least 20 years.

You can apply online using this link: https://www.gov.uk/doctoral-loan.

TIP

If you really want to pursue this area, don't let the course fees discourage you. The learning you will have on the courses and the training, both on the job and in the classroom, will provide you with key skills and competencies to become a great psychologist.

Difference between a PhD and a professional doctorate

Doctoral degrees include PhDs (research doctorates) and professional doctorates such as DClinPsy (Doctor of Clinical Psychology) or DPsych in Forensic Psychology. There is also another route to gaining a doctoral degree, PhD by publication, by submitting previously published works e.g., research papers, journal articles etc. A PhD is a doctoral degree but a professional doctorate isn't a PhD.

To qualify as a professional psychologist, e.g., clinical, forensic, sports and exercise etc. there are professional doctorates that combine research and taught modules and sometimes exams which provide key information, knowledge and practical placements.

These doctoral degrees are different from PhDs. PhDs are research postgraduate degrees that have fewer or no taught modules and are purely research-focused (Table 0.3).

Table 0.3 Difference between professional doctorate and a PhD

What is a PhD?	*What is a professional doctorate?*
Academic study, which is theory and research focused, in-depth study of a topic	Prepare practitioners for advanced professional practice in a specific field. The emphasis is on gaining expertise to address real-world problems and contribute to professional practice
The aim is to advance the field through researching something new	Assessment can include exams, course work and a research thesis
Usually no lectures, work is often solo under the guidance of supervisors	Usually lectures and modules with group and individual work, as well as placements and a Viva Voce at the end for the research thesis
Assessment is in the form of a written thesis varying in length of between 60 and 90,000 words long and at the end and a Viva Voce or a spoken exam at the end	Modules, placements with a cohort of learners
Can be done in any discipline, e.g., psychology, art, history, medicine	Examples – EdD – Doctor of Education, DBA – Doctor of Business Administration, DClinPsyc – Doctor of Clinical Psychology
Funding can be sought through research councils via universities or personally or through post graduate loads	Funding for certain doctorates such as DclinPsyc and DEdPsych is via the NHS or Department for Education
In the UK three to four years full-time up to eight part-time	Other professional doctorates may need to be funded personally via post graduate loans
	Three to four years full-time or up to eight years part-time

How do I choose my psychology specialism?

Now that you have read up to this point, you can understand how varied psychological careers are. You may feel intrigued or slightly overwhelmed by the numerous specialisations available in a career in psychology.

Understand your interests and where you want to work

To choose your specialism, there are a few things you need to understand. One of them is to know what things interest you, your values and the type of people you would like to work with. You will also need to understand which environments you would like to work in. Psychologists work primarily in public-sector environments, such as schools, the NHS, prisons, universities, local authorities, the civil service and councils. Additionally, organisational psychologists can work within any business or organisation and sports and exercise psychologists work with sports teams, athletes and organisations that support them (Figure 0.1).

Other careers you can pursue with a psychology degree

Those of you who are not interested in a career in the psychology field or applied psychology in general, this section is for you.

As the popularity of psychology careers increases, it is not to say that everyone wants or can access a career in psychology after pursuing a degree. There are several reasons for this.

- **Running out of steam** – for some people, a three- or four-year degree is enough and they may decide to give a psychology career a wide berth or take a break.
- **No longer interested** – After spending three or four years studying psychology, some people may feel like a career within applied psychology is not for them and they want to pursue other related or unrelated areas.

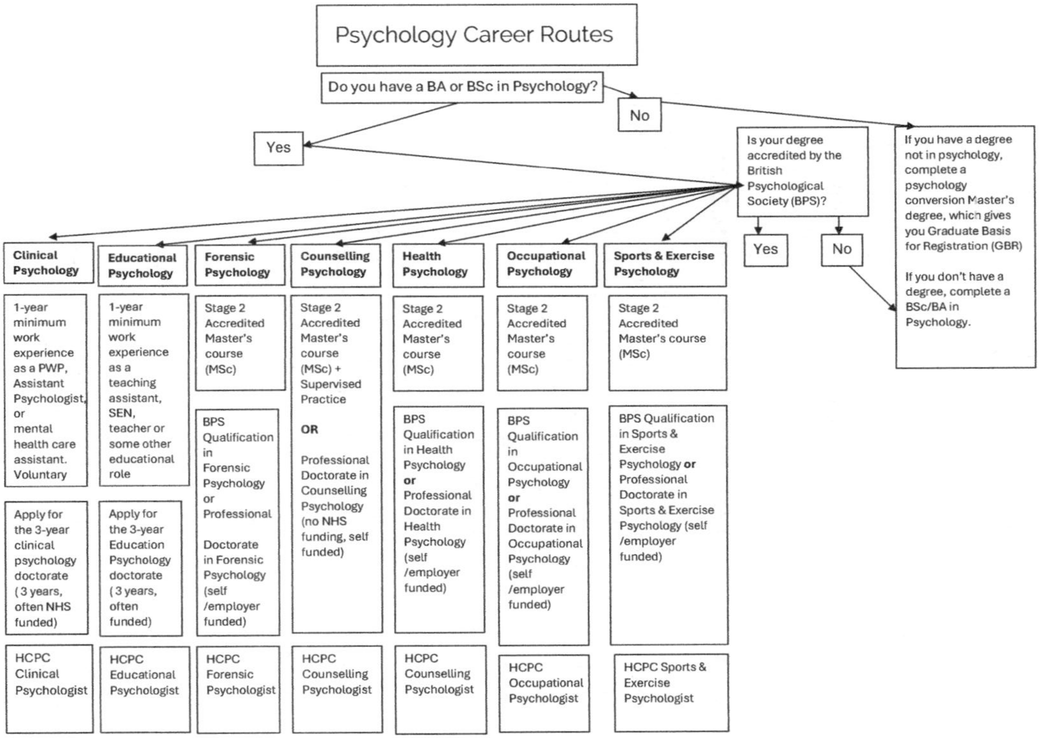

Figure 0.1 Psychology Career Routes Diagram

- **Can't afford access to further study** – the pathway to a career in psychology can be long and the cost of further study may be off-putting and a strong barrier for some people. For those who still want to pursue a career but still use some of the skills they developed from their undergraduate degrees.

This is something that needs to be addressed in psychology careers: the acknowledgement that the profession requires a significant amount of further study, often accompanied by a period of voluntary or low-paid work as a prerequisite.

DESTINATIONS FOR PSYCHOLOGY GRADUATES

According to a Prospects Luminate study[10] which looked at the destinations of graduates from 2024/2025, it found that out of over 18,000 students who had completed their first degree in 2021/2022 48.9% of psychology students were working full-time, 14.8% were working and studying, 8.6% were in further study and 6.5% were unemployed.

Those 1,905 who were in further study,

- 6.1% were completing a PhD, DPhil, MPhil or MRes.
- 15.3% were completing a postgraduate diploma or certificate including Postgraduate Certificate in Education (PGCE).
- 61.4% were completing a master's degree, either an MA or an MSc.
- 11.9% were completing a professional qualification.
- 5.2% were studying something else.

Those who were working were in roles including:

- Childcare, health and education occupations (20.4%).
- Legal, social, welfare professionals (12.5%).
- Clerical, secretarial and numerical clerks (11.6%).
- Retail, catering waiting and bar staff (11.5%).
- Health professionals (10.7%).

The top 10 professional jobs held by degree graduates in psychology included:

1. Welfare and housing professionals
2. Other psychologists
3. Human resources and industrial relations
4. Therapy professionals
5. Primary education teachers
6. Youth and community
7. Advertising and marketing
8. Secondary education teachers
9. Business and related research
10. Child and early years teachers

Key skills of a psychology graduate

Psychology courses provide students with various transferable skills, including planning and organisation, adaptability, research, analysis, collaboration and teamwork, evidence-based decision-making and written and verbal communication. These skills will be further explained below and how they relate to the undergraduate degree and beyond.

PLANNING AND ORGANISATION

Psychology students learn to plan and organise throughout their studies. This is mainly achieved through juggling multiple modules, planning research studies and participating in group work. Planning and organisational skills are crucial to every job; being able to stick to deadlines, plan your work and work independently are brilliant skills to acquire for any job.

ADAPTABILITY

Being able to work flexibly and adapt to different situations is also a vastly important skill you will learn during your psychological studies. Similar to planning and organisational skills, adaptability is a central skill needed for studying and the workplace. During your undergraduate and postgraduate studies, you will be juggling multiple projects and assignments to cover all the areas of psychology.

RESEARCH AND ANALYSIS

A core aspect of any social science, psychology notwithstanding, is the level of research and analysis. The research includes modules such as research methods, which teach students the differences between quantitative and qualitative research methods, including psychometric assessments, questionnaires, surveys, as well as interviews, ethnographic research and analysis, such as thematic analysis and statistical analysis, such as correlations. These skills are crucial if a person would like to go into further study in the psychology field and also provide great skills if you would like to go into user research, market research or marketing.

COLLABORATION AND TEAMWORK

Collaborating with others is a crucial aspect of any modern workplace. The ability to work across and between organisations is a key skill. During psychology degrees, this is also a key component, with students often doing group projects and assignments. Part of both psychology and non-psychology careers include cross-team and in-team collaboration, and developing this skill is very important.

EVIDENCE-BASED DECISION-MAKING

The term evidence-based refers to making decisions based on scientific research. Evidence-based decision-making is also about being practical and applying useful real-world knowledge to science. During your studies in psychology, almost everything you learn will be based on evidence, and you will learn how to assess, understand and talk about research and evidence. One example of evidence-based practice in psychology, specifically when it comes to clinical psychology, is the use of cognitive behavioural therapy as a treatment for anxiety and depression.

WRITTEN & VERBAL COMMUNICATION

Written and verbal communication is a key part of psychology degrees. Writing essays, understanding scientific research and communicating quantitative and qualitative data involve written and verbal skills. These skills are developed as part of a degree programme in psychology.

Other career routes for psychology graduates

Some people may choose to leave a career in applied psychology and pursue a completely different career path or direction. There are numerous roles that offer viable career paths for psychology graduates, leveraging skills developed and nurtured throughout their psychology studies. The roles below show some of many career paths for psychology graduates, outside of psychology.

ACCOUNT MANAGER

Account managers can be found in many industries, but particularly in client-facing ones where relationships are crucial. Account managers serve as the primary point of contact for customers, addressing queries, resolving problems and helping to upsell products and services. The skills required for this role include communication, business development, persuasion, project management, problem-solving and providing data insights on customer feedback.

ADVERTISING

People who work in advertising are involved in creating and delivering messages to promote services, products or ideas and work closely with clients to communicate these messages. Advertisers develop campaigns, create concepts and plan media output. They also manage clients, conduct market research and engage in creative work. The skills required for a role in advertising include communication, creative thinking, presenting ideas clearly and effectively, critical thinking, data analysis, teamwork, collaboration and problem-solving.

BUSINESS ANALYST

Business analysts help organisations maximise their effectiveness through data-driven decisions. The primary objective of a business analyst is to reduce costs and enhance effectiveness. Business analysts gather and analyse information and data, then make recommendations that help improve goals within an organisation. Business analysts make recommendations and design concrete action plans to make these recommendations more actionable. Business analysts require strong communication, analytical reasoning, problem-solving, data analysis and adaptability skills.

CAREERS ADVISOR

Careers advisors help people make informed decisions about education, training, careers and work, and assist them in navigating the workforce and achieving their professional goals.

Careers advisors need to research, explain educational and training opportunities and offer CV advice and other application support in individual, group or organisational settings. They work with job seekers, students and adult learners who are either employed or unemployed.

Careers advisors need to have good communication skills, be able to build rapport and motivate others, be flexible and adaptable, have emotional intelligence and empathy, be non-judgemental, research, plan, and organise, as well as analyse and solve problems. Career advisors can work in schools, universities, job and employment centres.

EXECUTIVE COACH

Executive coaches support leaders and managers to improve their skills, performance and effectiveness in their roles. Coaches can offer advice and guidance on further training to executives in areas such as communication, leadership skills, decision-making and emotional intelligence. Executive coaches develop leaders, enhance their performance and help them understand strategic skills, decision-making and communication skills that can be gained by people who complete a psychology undergraduate degree.

HUMAN RESOURCES

HR, or human resources, is primarily about finding, selecting and retaining the right people within an organisation. Talent is one of the most important aspects of running an organisation and HR professionals play a key role in the development of people and talent. HR professionals can work in a variety of different areas, including recruitment, training and development, employee relations or talent management. For HR roles, understanding people, communicating empathically and analysing and interpreting data are very important skills that can be gained from completing psychology studies.

MARKET RESEARCH

Market researchers collect, analyse and present both quantitative (working with numbers) and qualitative (creating stories out of data) information. Many market researchers work in agencies that undertake projects and consultancy work for other organisations, or they may be employed directly by these organisations. Market researchers need strong attention to detail, data analysis, planning and organisational skills, business and commercial awareness and flexibility. These skills can be developed while completing a psychology undergraduate degree.

SOCIAL WORK

Social workers support people and families, particularly those who are vulnerable, such as children and the elderly. Social workers work in many settings, including schools, hospitals and local councils. Social workers can choose to specialise in working with children, the elderly, those with disabilities, people who have substance abuse problems or people who may be homeless. Social workers support vulnerable individuals, provide information and support and make recommendations about courses of action for those in need. Social workers attend visits to people in need of support at their homes, as well as working in offices. The key skills that social workers need include empathy, understanding, communication, planning and organisation skills.

SPEECH AND LANGUAGE THERAPY

Speech and language therapists provide support for children and adults who find speech, eating, drinking and swallowing. Speech and language therapy is excellent for those who enjoy, or who are interested in science, language, linguistics and physiology. Speech and language therapy is varied, and practitioners can work in a variety of different settings. You will work with a multidisciplinary team. Speech and language therapists work with people who have learning disabilities, hearing impairments, cleft palates, stammer, selective mutism and speech and language difficulties because of strokes, Parkinson's disease and dementia. You can do a postgraduate course in speech and language therapy after an undergraduate degree in psychology. There is also a degree apprenticeship route, in which you study while working.

TEACHING

Teachers create healthy learning environments and monitor the development of children and young people. Teachers prepare and deliver lessons, research new topics, prepare students for exams, monitor learning and provide a holistic and effective learning environment.

Teachers need skills in teamwork, collaboration, listening, strong communication and resilience.

USER RESEARCH

User researchers collect, analyse and evaluate data and design websites, software and applications. User researchers plan and design user testing sessions, recruiting people to test software and other areas, such as websites. User researchers identify new product and design ideas and test those ideas. User researchers need skills including attention to detail, data analysis and interpretation, verbal and written communication skills. These professions are particularly well-suited for individuals who have completed their undergraduate degrees in psychology. They all draw on skills such as organisation, planning, teamwork, communication, data analysis and research skills.

Psychology career myths

This section will highlight common myths surrounding the career field of psychology. People have many misconceptions, ideas and inaccuracies about a psychology degree or postgraduate study and its applications.

1. This view leads me to my first myth, that **psychology is a 'Mickey Mouse/not a proper degree'**

   As you will see in the rest of this book, psychology is the study of human behaviour. This includes anyone studying psychology to learn about how people develop (developmental psychology), how people deal with health and disease (health psychology), how to motivate people to exercise and become more optimal athletes (sports and exercise psychology), how to support people's mental health and wellbeing (counselling and clinical psychology) as well as other applied areas including forensic, educational and organisational psychology.

   The undergraduate degree provides students with a solid foundation in research methods, critical thinking, planning, organisational skills, writing, communication and project management.

   Many people view psychology degrees as merely learning about common sense. However, the modules and the concepts are far from common knowledge. Modules include research methods, memory and decision-making, social psychology, language and cognition, health and clinical psychology, perception, the bias of science, sleep and circadian rhythms, psychopharmacology, genetics, psychology and education, sports and performance and ergonomics. The previous sentence isn't an exhaustive list but highlights that these modules aren't common sense; they are about learning theories and ideas about the human condition, synthesising those ideas and creating evidence-based practice and enquiry.

   These modules, which can be learned on an undergraduate psychology course or psychology conversion course, help you form a foundational understanding of people, biology, brain functions and psychology.

2. **You can only work in mental health with a psychology degree**
   The view that mental health, clinical or counselling psychology is the only route with a psychology degree isn't accurate. There are numerous other areas of applied psychology, as highlighted in this book, including health, forensic, sports, occupational, academic and educational psychology, which demonstrate the variety of routes within psychology itself. Beyond psychology, there are several careers and areas to pursue with a psychology undergraduate degree, such as sales, marketing, advertising, market research and user research; academia and teaching are also options.
3. **Psychology and psychiatry are the same**
   Psychology is the study of human behaviour, and psychiatry is a medical specialism focusing on treating mental disorders such as schizophrenia and emotionally unstable personality disorder. Psychologists who work within mental health (forensic, clinical and counselling psychologists) complete a professional doctorate to practise and work with people. In contrast, psychiatrists are medical doctors who do a degree in medicine and after their foundation training specialise in psychiatry. Psychiatrists can prescribe medication for mental health conditions such as antidepressants and anti-anxiety medication, whereas psychologists can't. Even though both clinical, counselling and forensic psychologists work within the mental health field, they are not the same as psychiatrists because psychiatrists are medical doctors.
4. **Psychologists can read your mind and know what you are thinking**
   This myth is another one that gets spread around often. One of the underlying thoughts is that somehow psychologists are 'mind readers' and are constantly analysing people. Psychologists don't learn this at any stage during their training. The portrayal of psychologists in popular culture is to blame for this myth. Clinical, counselling, sports and exercise and forensic psychologists use rigorous research techniques, models and training to understand and connect with clients. Psychologists can understand patterns in thoughts and thinking but they cannot literally read minds.

What to do if you get a 2:2 or a third-class degree at undergraduate level?

What if you get a 2:2

Someone who gets a 2:2 at undergraduate level will have obtained an average of 50% across all of their modules usually. For a lot of graduate schemes and master's degree they would prefer a 2:1 grade (an average of 60% across modules) entry criteria, but this isn't always a hard-and-fast rule. With some work experience and possibly a master's degree, this can greatly increase your chances of getting onto a professional doctorate, PhD programme or graduate programme.

For graduate programmes for careers outside of psychology, organisations such as Ernst and Young and PWC are more flexible when applying criteria to applicants for their graduate scheme. They will have some assessments instead, which will act as a measure for applicants. Additionally, graduate programmes such as Police Now and Enterprise Rent-A-Car will accept applications from those who have a 2:2. Some Procter & Gamble schemes, the Civil Service Fast Stream and the NHS graduate programme also accept applications from those with a 2:2.

What if you get a third-class degree?

A third-class degree is when you average 40% across all modules, and this is still a passing grade. For some graduate programmes and further study, a third-class degree may not allow you to be considered for some roles. Checking with each scheme or postgraduate course may be pertinent here to understand what a third-class degree means for your future career. If you do want to pursue further study in psychology and you do obtain a third-class degree, according to the BPS, if you started your degree from 2006 onwards you wouldn't be eligible for Graduate Basis for Chartered Membership (GBC) which allows you to go further through the psychology careers route. To be able to continue with a third-class you would need to undertake a psychology conversion course which are often master's degrees that you can undertake in one or two years, before moving on to your specialism of choice.

How to use this book

The introductory chapter was to help your thinking about the background of psychology courses, how diverse the courses are at undergraduate level and an introduction to the applied areas of psychology. Each of the subsequent chapters will go through areas of applied psychology including clinical, educational, forensic, counselling, health, occupational, sports and exercise psychology. The book also goes into other associated pathways such as clinical associate psychologist and psychological wellbeing practitioner.

NOTES

1 https://www.britannica.com/science/applied-psychology.
2 Health and Care Professionals Council (2020). Diversity data report 2021. https://www.hcpc-uk.org/resources/reports/2021/diversity-data-report-2021/.
3 Kancelijak, D., & Calia, C. (2023). Section 1: Human rights and professional engagement. Diversity and inclusion in UK psychology: A nationwide survey. *Clinical Psychology Forum*, 369, 25–29.
4 https://www.hee.nhs.uk/our-work/mental-health/psychological-professions/improving-equity-inclusion-people-access-psychological-professions-training.
5 https://portal.bps.org.uk/Accredited-Courses.
6 https://www.gov.uk/student-finance/who-qualifies.
7 https://www.gov.uk/check-what-undergraduate-student-finance-you-can-apply-for-depending-on-your-nationality-and-residency.
8 https://www.ucas.com/money-and-student-life/money/scholarships-grants-and-bursaries.
9 https://study-uk.britishcouncil.org/scholarships-funding/commonwealth-scholarships.
10 What do graduates do? 2024/2025 produced by Prospects (part of Jisc) and AGCAS. https://graduatemarkettrends.cdn.prismic.io/graduatemarkettrends/aQ4HjLpReVYa4PSy_what-do-graduates-do-2024.pdf

1

CLINICAL PSYCHOLOGY

WHAT IS CLINICAL PSYCHOLOGY?

When people think of psychology, they often envision a psychologist taking notes while a patient lies on a couch. This view of psychology and therapy is so ingrained in our psyches, and it can give a narrow idea of what a psychologist is and what the discipline does. Clinical psychologists often deal with a variety of mental health concerns and conditions.

Clinical psychologists often use diagnostic assessments, interviews and other validated methods to understand people. These can include addiction, anxiety, depression, relationship problems and eating disorders. Clinical psychologists can work with clients/patients of any age who have behavioural, emotional or psychological distress.

Clinical psychologists aim to reduce distress and promote psychological wellbeing, enabling people to access services and engage in meaningful relationships. Clinical psychologists also provide treatment using cognitive behavioural therapy (CBT), which is now available through UK National Health Service (NHS). Clinical psychologists can work in academia, teaching and research alongside the NHS, or privately in private practice. Clinical psychologists can also be found working in hospitals,

DOI: 10.4324/9781003669449-2

clinics, health centres, community mental health teams, social services, schools, prisons and NHS IAPT (Improving Access to Psychological Therapies) services. Clinical psychology is one of the most sought-after specialisms for people pursuing a career in psychology.

TRAINING

The process of becoming a clinical psychologist in the UK can seem quite long and arduous. The first step is getting on British Psychological Society's accredited undergraduate degree and these typically last either three or four years (if you do a degree with a work placement element). Undergraduate degrees in psychology cover a range of topics including memory, social psychology, statistics and research methods, language, neuropsychology, learning and developmental psychology. Often, courses are assessed by exams, essays, presentations and research projects.

As competition to gain a place in a clinical psychology doctoral programme is quite high, entry requirements include a 2.1 or higher at the undergraduate level, along with relevant work experience. As clinical psychology is becoming increasingly competitive, many people are pursuing master's degrees after their undergraduate degrees in topics such as clinical psychology, foundations of clinical psychology, child and adolescent mental health, clinical mental health sciences and developmental psychology and clinical practice. It is not a requirement to complete postgraduate studies and if it is something you don't want to do or don't have the finances to do, you can gain valuable experience and preparation for the doctorate in other ways.

The professional doctorate itself will focus on you learning CBT and at least one other therapy modality. You will learn how to apply knowledge and theory to different client groups including patients, staff and to assist organisational change. You will also learn how to apply research methods to research design.

WHAT WORK EXPERIENCE DO I NEED?

The work experience needed to gain a place on a clinical doctorate programme can be gained from varied settings. Self-awareness and reflection are very important aspects of becoming a clinical psychologist, so starting this early in your journey can stand you in good stead for the future. Some clinical doctoral courses specify the length of experience required, e.g., 12 months before an application to the doctoral programme is considered.

The experience needed to gain a place in the doctorate can be full or part-time, voluntary or paid in a variety of settings, including charities and private work. In the NHS, with social services, as a support worker or health care assistant work. Working as a research assistant at a university or other settings can also count as valuable experience. Other types of experience that may help towards gaining a place on the clinical doctorate include training as a psychological wellbeing practitioner (PWP), clinical associate psychologist (CAP) or assistant psychologist roles. Previously, assistant psychologist roles were seen as one of the only viable ways to gain a place on a clinical doctorate and thus, competition for those roles was very high. However, with the advent of the PWP and the Clinical Associate apprenticeship roles, there are other viable routes, as well as pursuing mental health care assistant roles and other roles within health care settings.

THE CLINICAL PSYCHOLOGY DOCTORATE

The clinical psychology doctorate lasts three years full-time and is offered by 30 universities in the UK. The course offers research and classroom-based learning as well as on-the-job clinical training in NHS settings. People on the courses spend around 50% of their time in clinical practice and the rest in teaching, research and academic workshops hosted by experienced local clinicians.

Courses vary, but a typical week can include one day of teaching, one day of study and three days of placement. Assessments can include assignments and exams, depending on the course. Research is also conducted in the second and third year of the programme and is often written up as a doctoral thesis.

WHAT DO YOU LEARN ON THE CLINICAL PSYCHOLOGY DOCTORATE?

Many courses will include the following core modules:

- **Assessment and formulation** – which is about understanding and using psychological assessments to understand clients and patients more deeply, developing case formulations across different groups, i.e. children, adults and those with learning disabilities.
- **Intervention approaches** – these modules include CBT, systematic and family therapy, psychodynamic therapy, acceptance and commitment therapy and compassion-focussed therapy. These modules focus on the theories and their practical applications.
- **Common and complex mental health conditions** – the next area you will focus on is learning about mental health and psychiatric disorders such as psychosis, anxiety, depression, post-traumatic stress disorder (PTSD), and this may overlap with learning about other areas of psychology like health and neuropsychology.
- **Psychological theory and practice** – these modules highlight the theory, science and ethical aspects of clinical psychology.

Other courses may also focus on aspects such as diversity, inclusion, power and reflective practice.

Another important aspect of the Doctor of Clinical Psychology are the placements. Trainees will do several six-month core placements within the NHS and will be in areas including:

- Adult mental health
- Child and adolescent mental health
- Older adults
- People with disabilities

There may also be modules throughout the course that overlap with areas such as health or neuropsychology. Another aspect of the doctorate is the research. Each individual in their final year will be expected to produce a doctoral thesis around an original area and show research skills and evidence-based practice.

FUNDING FOR DOCTORATES IN CLINICAL PSYCHOLOGY COURSES

As discussed in the previous chapter, the NHS provides funding for most places on clinical psychology doctorates. People accepted onto NHS courses are employed as trainee clinical psychologists while they study. Those in funded places start their training with a salary on a Band 6 of £37,338, which is the bottom of Band 6. The NHS then pays course fees for the trainees.

SELF-FUNDED PLACES FOR INTERNATIONAL STUDENTS

The self-funded route is specifically for international students. Fees vary but are around £17,000–36,500 per year and entry requirements are the same as for funded places.

International students can apply to doctoral courses. International students are only eligible for self-funded places at some universities within the UK. These universities include University College London (UCL), Kings College London, University of Bath, University of East Anglia, University of Manchester and University of Exeter.

WHAT'S THE REALITY?

This route to psychology is competitive, and in 2020, 18% of applicants gained a place on the clinical doctorate. Being able to support your application with practical and research experience is very important. If you can get some research assistant experience during your undergraduate degree, if you have the ability and funds to pursue a research master's or volunteer to work on research projects whilst working, it can really help you.

If you feel like this route is not for you, there are plenty of alternative roles and routes to clinical psychology (some are highlighted above) and there are ways you can work clinically to enhance mental health and encourage wellbeing. These roles include becoming a psychotherapist, counsellor, wellbeing professional, social worker or many other roles.

CASE STUDY,

Dr Nancy Nsiah, clinical psychologist

Dr Nancy Nsiah is a clinical psychologist who currently works at Guys and St Thomas' hospital London.

Nancy completed her undergraduate degree at the University of Surrey where she also completed a placement year as part of the course. During her time on her placement, she was an honorary assistant psychologist in the South London and Maudsley NHS trust, where she worked at a brain injury unit and completed a literature review for a research publication. She then worked as an independent mental health advocate at Rethink Mental Illness. In this role, she assisted individuals who had been sectioned under the Mental Health Act or those who had a community treatment order. Nancy helped people become aware of their rights and assisted their decision-making process by using listening, motivating and empathy. She enabled patients to feel more empowered in their recovery journey. These roles were prior to her admission to the clinical psychology doctorate programme.

Since qualifying, Nancy has also started her own initiative called the Art of Being Well, where she mentors aspiring clinical psychologists from racially minoritised groups and also delivers mental health workshops, training and consultancy to private organisations and community groups.

Dr Nancy Nsiah chose clinical psychology for a variety of reasons:

> Growing up I was encouraged to pursue medicine, but to be honest I was not keen on touching people! Within my community people commonly spoke about physical symptoms such as headaches but would deny the existence of 'stress' or 'anxiety.' The stigma around mental health reinforced a separation between mind and body which I felt were inextricably linked. This planted a seed for me to pursue a career in clinical Psychology.

The advice she would give anyone interested in pursuing clinical psychology:

> Gain an in-depth understanding about what clinical psychologists do – it's more than therapy! Recognising the multiple components of the role can help you identify valuable work experience and expand your thinking around the possible areas where you can build these skills.
>
> You can get an understanding of the roles by looking at job adverts and descriptions for qualified clinical psychologists, networking with clinical psychologists and reading 'A day in the life', style articles on the psychologists magazine website... there is more than one way or one route to be coming a clinical psychologist - future your journey to suit your interests!

Dr Nancy Nsiah's career timeline

Highly Specialist Clinical Psychologist | Guys and St Thomas' NHS Foundation Trust | Sept 2021–present

Visiting Lecturer | Various Institutions | Present

Director and Founder | The Art of Being Well | Feb 2019–present

Clinical Psychologist | Great Ormond Street | Dec 2017–2022

Trainee Clinical Psychologist | Surrey and Boarders NHS Trust | Sept 2014–Sept 2017 – several placements inducing adults, learning disability, older adults, child placement and a specialist eating disorders service.

University of Surrey | Doctorate in Clinical Psychology (PsyD) | 2014–2017

Rethink Mental Illness | Independent Mental Health Advocate | June 2011–Sept 2014

Placement year | Honorary Assistant Psychologist | South London and Maudsley NHS Trust, projects at the Brain Injury Unit and was working on the Beresford project. This project was to assist those who had complex substance misuse-related problems | 2009–2010

University of Surrey | BSc Psychology | 2007–2011 including a placement year

ALTERNATIVE ROLES RELATED TO CLINICAL PSYCHOLOGY CAREERS

Psychological wellbeing practitioner

PWPs or psychological wellbeing practitioners are trained to work in NHS settings to help people and support those who experience 'common' mental health problems such as anxiety and depression. Practitioners allow patients to self-manage their conditions using low-intensity and high-intensity evidence-based interventions based on cognitive and behavioural theories. The PWP role was originally developed to work within Improving Access to Psychological Therapies (IAPT) services in England. These services are designed to increase psychological improvement and social inclusion in people who have mild to medium cases of anxiety and depression. PWPs are usually the first mental health practitioner someone would see, for those who require access to psychological therapies in the NHS. If the initial form of interventions that PWPs administer is unsuitable, clients will be recommended for other types of assistance.

A psychological wellbeing practitioner role can be useful for gaining a place on the clinical doctoral course because it mainly involves working in NHS settings and dealing with general practitioners (GPs) and other medical professionals. A significant component of clinical psychology training involves working alongside various professionals with caseloads. Therefore, the PWP role gives a good insight into a clinical psychologist's work as part of a multidisciplinary team.

CLINICAL ASSOCIATE IN PSYCHOLOGY

This role is fairly new in the NHS and clinical associates are mental health professionals whose duties include assessing, formulating and treating patients with specific conditions. Clients are either in care or adult mental health settings or in areas involving young people and families. Clinical associates operate in certain specialised areas and are supervised by qualified practitioner psychologists. To become a clinical associate, you need to complete a British Psychological Society (BPS)–accredited undergraduate course in psychology or a conversion course, followed by an MSc in Psychological Therapies in primary care or applied psychology for children and young people.

If you have completed either a PWP role or a CAP role as highlighted above, you can't apply for a clinical psychology professional doctorate straight away. This is because both the PWP and the CAP roles are funded by the NHS for the training portion. You will have to be in these roles for two years before you apply for the clinical psychology doctorate places.

ASSISTANT PSYCHOLOGISTS

Assistant psychologist (AP) roles are often seen as the traditional precursor to the clinical doctoral training. Assistant psychologists are employed by the NHS, but also in forensic and non-profit sectors and are often involved in preparing or administering psychological assessments, observing and recording behavioural observations, implementing treatment and intervention programmes, researching and gathering information.

Assistant psychologists are usually supervised by practitioner psychologists, and you will receive ongoing supervision that will help you engage in self-reflection and self-awareness. Assistant psychologists are usually paid at an NHS Band 4 or Band 5 wage. It is important for those who want to pursue this route to have skills including knowledge of psychological theory, an interest in understanding human behaviour, sympathy and empathy, good planning and organisational skills and adaptability and flexibility. To apply for AP roles, you will need to have an undergraduate degree in psychology accredited by the BPS.

WHAT DO ASSISTANT PSYCHOLOGISTS DO?

Assistant psychologists can do a variety of things such as providing care for clients and patients, carry out assessments, research and analysis or doing administrative tasks for multidisciplinary teams.

OTHER ROLES

The roles listed below are relatively recent additions to NHS mental health services. These roles combine work and study for 12 months and people will work closely with other mental health practitioners and receive a graduate/postgraduate certificate. These roles are currently being piloted across England. Mostly, people will spend one day a week studying, mostly remotely and the rest working and gaining experience in a role. These roles are fully funded, and people receive a Band 4 salary whilst training which often increase to Band 5 salary whilst qualified. To apply for these roles, you will need to search for the roles and then apply to the required training institute for the learning aspect.

YOUTH INTENSIVE PSYCHOLOGICAL PRACTITIONER

Youth intensive psychological practitioners provide assessments and interventions for people aged 13–17 who have severe mental health challenges and needs. The patients are usually inpatients, and the role is there to help young people recover and help them live full and fruitful lives.

Individuals will work closely with clinical psychologists and other health care practitioners to assess and formulate treatments and psychologically informed solutions. People need to have a psychology undergraduate degree and a minimum of a 2:2 grade on an accredited undergraduate degree that gives you Graduate Basis for Chartered membership or GBC to train as a youth intensive psychological practitioner. You will need to apply for a position as a trainee youth intensive psychological practitioner and the training is funded as at a Band 4 rate, increasing to a Band 5 NHS rate once qualified. You will need good communication skills, experience of working with people who need mental health support, either in a paid or voluntary role and good interpersonal skills.

CHILDREN'S WELLBEING PRACTITIONER

These professionals are trained to assess and support children and young people with mild to moderate symptoms of anxiety, depression and other behavioural problems. Children's wellbeing practitioners offer and give young people interventions that are based on CBT and self-help techniques. Children's wellbeing practitioners also support parents and carers. To apply to train as a children's wellbeing practitioner, experience with children and young people is important.

EDUCATION MENTAL HEALTH PRACTITIONER

These practitioners work across education and healthcare to provide mental health support to children and young people in schools and colleges. The training will focus on helping children and young people navigate what's called common mental health conditions such as mild to moderate anxiety, depression and behavioural problems.

You will use cognitive therapy-based support to address any mental health needs. Your training will also involve supporting schools and colleges with organisational approaches that can embed and support wellbeing. As part of your role, you could be advising children on how to cope with panic or anxiety attacks, teaching young people how to manage anxiety and depression, promoting an emotionally healthy organisation and creating ways to give young people and children the right support.

Your training will be fully funded and you will be employed at the same time and receive a salary. To be eligible to apply for this role, you will need teamwork and interpersonal skills, relationship building, understanding of the education system, understanding of mental health issues, written and verbal communication, problem-solving, and time management skills.

You don't have to have a degree to do this role and you can find these roles on the NHS website under trainee education mental health practitioner. The training is 12 months, which combines both theory and practice, self-study and work placements. You will be employed by a healthcare organisation but will work around educational settings like schools and colleges, specialist schools or pupil referral units for people aged 5–18. You will also receive supervision throughout your training and will be supported by other staff.

MENTAL HEALTH AND WELLBEING PRACTITIONER

These professionals provide wellbeing- focussed psychologically informed interventions and coordinate care for adults with serious mental health problems. These roles are based in the community and are for people who want to support adults to live their lives more effectively. You will be seeing people who have been referred by their GPs and other services, and you will help decide what the best support will be for them.

You will help people with their problem-solving, sleep, recognising emotions, building confidence and supporting them in managing medicine and other things. Mental health and wellbeing practitioners work with interdisciplinary teams to promote recovery.

The training is one year and one day a week will be spent on study and the remaining time will be for undertaking tasks in a community mental health service. When you are qualified, you will spend about half your working week (around 20 hours) seeing patients in the clinic, at their homes or online.

The skills you will need include excellent teamwork and interpersonal skills, understanding mental health, written and verbal communication skills, problem-solving and creativity, time management and flexibility.

You don't need a degree to apply for this trainee role, but you need to apply for a position as a trainee mental health and wellbeing practitioner. The role is fully funded, and you will earn a Band 4 salary when training.

HOW TO APPLY FOR THESE ROLES

These roles are often advertised on the NHS jobs website based in specific areas. The standard NHS jobs portal will ask for a CV/application form along with a cover letter/application question to try and understand your motivation for applying to these roles.

CHAPTER SUMMARY

- Clinical psychology is one of the most popular undergraduate pathways for students.
- There are many pathways to entering a clinical doctorate programme to become a clinical psychologist after an undergraduate degree in psychology. After an undergraduate degree, pathways to a career in clinical psychology include becoming a PWP, AP, CAP, mental health care assistant and a host of other related roles.
- Competition for a place on the clinical psychology doctorate is quite high; however, with the right experience, there is still a chance to get on the programme.
- The clinical psychology doctoral degree is a funded pathway, and courses are funded by the NHS but some do accept self-funded routes.
- Even if you are interested in a career in any of these areas without completing the doctorate, you can still have a fulfilling career as a PWP, CAP, AP or mental health care assistant; it's all dependent on your personal preference.

2

NEUROPSYCHOLOGY

Neuropsychology is a postgraduate specialism to focus on after qualifying as a clinical, counselling or educational psychologist. Neuropsychologists work with people who have had traumatic brain injuries, strokes, brain tumours or neurodegenerative conditions such as Alzheimer's disease and movement disorders such as Parkinson's disorder. They also understand how these conditions affect behaviour, mood and cognitive skills. Ultimately, they assess individuals' capacity and then suggest treatment plans to support their day-to-day activities. A neuropsychologist requires clinical knowledge and extensive additional training and a solid understanding of neuroscience.

Neuropsychology is split into two areas, clinical neuropsychology and cognitive neuropsychology. Clinical neuropsychology involves assessing and rehabilitating individuals with brain injuries, neurodevelopmental conditions or neurological diseases. Clinical neuropsychologists assess domains such as attention, concentration, processing speed, language, learning and memory, reasoning, problem-solving, mood, personality and spatial awareness. They are trained to understand the link between the brain and behaviour. These things are assessed for

DOI: 10.4324/9781003669449-3

a variety of reasons; it could be to create a report to support a person's return to work or study, or to assess the overall impact of a condition. Additionally, an assessment may be needed to assess a person's ability for medical treatment.

Clinical neuropsychologists also use rehabilitation techniques, such as problem-solving training and strategies to improve memory and understanding. People who specialise in neuropsychology have a background as chartered clinical, counselling or educational psychologists and then choose to further specialise in neuropsychology.

Clinical neuropsychologists work within hospitals, community organisations, prisons, private practice, charities, schools and the criminal justice system. Clinical neuropsychologists work with doctors, psychiatrists, nurses and social workers in a multidisciplinary way.

Contrastingly, cognitive neuropsychology is more focused on the research side of neuropsychology. Cognitive neuropsychologists conduct research to understand how the brain functions under injury or disease and don't work directly with patients, as clinical neuropsychologists do. Cognitive neuropsychologists are more likely to work in universities or research institutions.

ROUTE TO BE A CLINICAL NEUROPSYCHOLOGIST

As this is a postgraduate specialism, clinical neuropsychologists would typically need to be chartered educational, clinical or counselling psychologists and have obtained a professional doctorate.

The British Psychological Society has a special qualification route for those who want to obtain a qualification. The qualification is called QiCN (Qualification in Clinical Neuropsychology) and provides a competency framework for those practising as neuropsychologists. On completion, people become full members of the Division of Neuropsychology. The qualification takes two years to complete and you need to be in a suitable post to allow you to gain relevant experience.

SALARY

Clinical neuropsychologists can get paid anything from £55,000 to £74,000 per year in an National Health Service (NHS) role and possibly more if in private practice.

WHAT WORK EXPERIENCE DO I NEED?

As this route is a post-qualification route, the work experience element is different. People would need to be employed in a clinical or educational role where they are working to support those with brain injuries. Most of these roles would be in an NHS or private healthcare service or maybe a charity, focusing on work with those who have neurological disorders and diseases.

HOW DO I KNOW IF THIS ROUTE IS FOR ME?

If you are interested in how the brain functions, especially with people who have had neurological injuries and you want to support people in a more direct way, this route is for you.

CHAPTER SUMMARY

- Neuropsychology focuses on individuals who have had traumatic brain injuries, strokes, brain tumours or other brain trauma.
- Neuropsychology is split into two areas, clinical and cognitive neuropsychology. Clinical neuropsychologists focus on assessing and rehabilitating individuals, evaluating memory, processing speed, attention span and other cognitive domains. Clinical neuropsychologists often work within hospital and healthcare settings.
- To qualify as a neuropsychologist, you would need to be a qualified clinical, counselling or educational psychologist and then specialise in neuropsychology afterwards by completing the British Psychological Society (BPS) QiCN (Qualification in Clinical Neuropsychology), which allows

learners to understand key competencies. This qualification takes two years to complete.

- Clinical neuropsychology is an area for those who are interested in rehabilitation and working with people with brain injuries, as well as those who are interested in working with multidisciplinary teams including clinical psychologists, nurses and medical doctors.

3

CHILD AND ADOLESCENT PSYCHOTHERAPY

INTRODUCTION

This related area is little-known but is also an interesting mental health career pathway. Child and adolescent psychotherapists work with children and young people and their families to treat a range of psychological problems. These practitioners primarily use psychoanalytic psychotherapy and include methods such as talking, playing, drawing and talking to families, carers and other professionals. You will be working with Children and Young People's Mental Health Services (CYPMHS). These teams work in an interdisciplinary way with children's services, education, mental health services, clinical psychologists and social services. This route can be an alternative route for those who may not want to pursue clinical or educational psychology.

TRAINING

The qualification route to be a child and adolescent psychotherapist is as follows:

- This route is a postgraduate route.
- Undergraduate degree: in psychology, counselling, social work, nursing, education or a related subject.

DOI: 10.4324/9781003669449-4

- A preclinical training course: these courses include extended psychoanalytic infant and young child observations, work discussion seminars, psychoanalytic theory and child development. The courses are self-funded, but bursaries are sometimes available. Preclinical training equips everyone with the skills necessary to progress further, such as emotional availability and self-awareness. The Association for Child Psychotherapists (ACP) accredits seven preclinical training courses across the UK.
- As part of this preclinical training experience, working with children and young people in various settings, such as schools, healthcare, social care and other sectors, must be gained.
- These courses can be around one to two years full-time and more if you pursue the course part-time. Fees also vary.
- Additionally, personal psychoanalysis a minimum of three times a week is encouraged but not a hard selection criteria.
- Funding can also be obtained via postgraduate student loans if you are doing an MSc programme, bank loans or working and bursaries and scholarships may be available.

CLINICAL TRAINING

After your preclinical training course, you can then apply for the professional doctorate in child and adolescent psychotherapy. This professional doctorate is also a National Health Service (NHS)–funded course. In England, there is a National Child and Adolescent Psychotherapy Training scheme funded by Health Education England. Different funding agreements are in place for Scotland, Northern Ireland and Wales.

To qualify as a child and adolescent psychotherapist, the clinical training course is four years long and this includes teaching, supervision, personal psychoanalysis and a salaried training post with an NHS Trust (at Band 6). Part-time options may also be available.

The training includes an extensive grasp of child development, psychopathology and psychoanalytic, psychotherapeutic technique connected to the trainee's direct work experience on placement with clients aged between 0 and 25 years old. There are five training schools across the United Kingdom, including Birmingham, Glasgow, Leeds and two in London.

HOW MUCH WILL YOU EARN?

During training, you will be on a Band 6 NHS pay scale (starting at £38,636–46,581), and once qualified, you will progress to a Band 7 pay scale (£46,148–54,710).

KEY SKILLS

- Self-awareness and reflection
- Empathy
- Curiosity
- Communication
- Teamwork and collaboration
- Resilience and maturity

WHERE YOU'LL WORK

- Children and Young People's Mental Health Services (CYPMHS)
- Hospital teams
- Eating disorder teams
- Perinatal and pre-infant services
- Schools
- Forensic services

CHAPTER SUMMARY

- Child and adolescent psychotherapy is related to supporting children and young people through psychological conditions and mental distress. This route is open to those who have completed undergraduate degrees in psychology, but other degrees such as nursing, counselling and social work.
- Child and adolescent psychotherapy training includes completing an undergraduate degree, enrolling on a preclinical

training year and applying for a funded doctorate in child and adolescent psychotherapy. This course is also funded by the NHS in the UK.

- After qualification, individuals can work within NHS often with other health care professionals including forensic and clinical psychologists, social workers, nurses and doctors as well as schools.

4

EDUCATIONAL PSYCHOLOGY

You may have heard of this specialism, but you may be unsure what educational psychology is or what educational psychologists do. Educational psychology is the application of psychological theory and research to provide practical solutions and interventions that support children, young people and their families in educational settings, e.g., schools, colleges and universities. These practical solutions and interventions aim to promote educational and psychological wellbeing in learning settings. Some of these interventions and solutions may also be used to assist people who are neurodiverse or who have specific additional needs and the interventions can enable them to achieve their potential. Educational psychologists complete assessments, monitor and evaluate interventions or techniques with children and young people.

Educational psychologists conduct observations and interpret assessments to identify needs and use interventions to help children and young people overcome difficulties. These interventions can include specialised learning programmes, behavioural management techniques or relaxation methods. Often, educational psychologists work with social workers, doctors and anyone involved in children's education.

DOI: 10.4324/9781003669449-5

WHAT QUALIFICATIONS DO I NEED?

To practise as a qualified educational psychologist in the UK, you will need an undergraduate degree in psychology, accredited by the British Psychological Society (BPS). The next step is to complete a three-year accredited doctoral degree in educational psychology. These doctoral degrees are mostly funded doctoral courses and there are currently over ten universities available to study for a doctorate in educational psychology in the UK. UK Department of Education funds the course and it covers tuition fees for all three years and a bursary for the first year of study. Gaining a place on the educational psychology doctorate does require candidates to have relevant work experience after completing an undergraduate degree in psychology. The next section will shed some light on what that experience is.

WHAT WORK EXPERIENCE WILL HELP ME GAIN ADMISSION TO THE EDUCATIONAL PSYCHOLOGY DOCTORATE PROGRAMME?

Universities expect candidates to have a minimum of one year's full-time experience working with children and young people within a variety of settings, including education, childcare or youth justice. This can include paid employment or a combination of voluntary and part-time experiences, which add up to one year of full-time experience. This is equivalent to 37 hours per week over a 52-week period. Universities often like knowledge and understanding of the education system and also people who are aware of the application of psychological theories to educational settings.

Previously, trainee educational psychologists were required to undertake teacher training after completing their undergraduate degrees in psychology and to become teachers for a number of years before applying for the educational psychology doctorate. However, this requirement has been changed. Roles that count as relevant experience to get onto the doctorate include roles like education social worker, social work assistant psychologist, teaching assistant, learning mentor, careers advisor, care worker, early years worker or speech and language therapist.

HOW CAN I GET FUNDING FOR MY DOCTORATE?

Local authorities organise funding for the doctorate in educational psychology once a place has been gained on the doctoral course. In the first year, the university you are attached to will pay your bursary directly, the amount is £16,266 if your course is outside London and £16,715 if your course is within London. After the first year, the funding arrangements vary, but you are paid either a bursary amount or a paid salary.

SELF-FUNDING

Some universities offer self-funded places and each university will decide this. This is also the process if you are an international student and therefore not eligible to receive government funding for the course. If self-funding is an option you would like to explore further, please contact the university/universities directly. The educational psychology-funded training scheme is currently the only scheme that funds educational psychologists in the UK, unless self-funding is an option. If you choose to self-fund, you still need to be able to pay the fees and also meet the selection criteria of the different universities you are applying to.

SKILLS NEEDED

The skills you will need to be a successful student and practitioner of educational psychology include negotiation, self-awareness, compassion, consulting, assessment, research, interpretation, verbal and written communication, prioritisation, evaluation, teamwork and collaboration. These skills are gathered from the various studies you will undertake along with the work experience you will gather before your course and the work you will do during your doctorate.

HOW DO I KNOW IF EDUCATIONAL PSYCHOLOGY IS FOR ME?

If you are interested in children and young people, education, empowering others, working with others and communicating with professionals, this career is for you. You may not be working as directly and hands-on with children or young people, but you will be collaborating with interdisciplinary teams to develop interventions and strategies that help children and young people thrive within education.

WHAT'S THE REALITY?

As this is a funded route, it is also competitive. Being able to demonstrate both practical and research experience when applying to the doctorate programme is important. If you can do a master's degree before you apply, it can help you decide if it's a route you want to go down and provide you with additional research experience. If this is not a reality for you, there are plenty of ways you can develop and amass experience through working full-time in schools, tutoring centres, youth clubs, pupil referral units or nurseries. If you start along this route and become disheartened or frustrated, there are plenty of ways you can apply psychology to educational settings and bring value to many people's lives.

WHAT WILL I LEARN ON THE EDUCATIONAL PSYCHOLOGY DOCTORATE?

The core modules on an educational psychology professional doctorate include

- **Child and adolescent development** – which go through theories and research about learning, how people process information or cognition, social development and emotional development from 0 to 25.
- **Assessment and formulation** – these modules highlight psychological assessment of children and young people.

- **Intervention and consulting** – this involves the trainee learning evidence-based interventions such as social-emotional learning, including social awareness, relationship skills and decision-making. Additionally, this could also encompass therapeutic techniques such as Cognitive Behavioural Therapy (CBT) and play therapy.
- **Partnership working** – learning how to collaborate with other stakeholders such as teachers, social workers and carers to support the child or young person.
- **Frameworks for practice** – this involves keeping abreast of legal, ethical and systemic processes, as well as safeguarding and promoting children's rights and wellbeing.
- **Learning and social environmental factors** – this focuses on understanding how the environment, school, family and peer groups can affect children and young people's behaviour.
- **Research methods** – research methods form the core of many psychology courses. This includes critical analysis, literature reviews and primary and secondary research. Additionally, conducting a final thesis is also a core part of the doctorate.
- **Placements** – as with clinical psychology, there are many practical placements trainees do as part of the doctorate. This can be around three days a week during the duration of the doctorate.

ASSOCIATED ROLES

Assistant educational psychologist

The assistant educational psychologist roles are psychology graduates who work with qualified educational psychologists within educational psychology services. To do this role, people often have experience working with children and young people. People in this role work with schools, families and young people through observations, consultations and evidence-based interventions. They also work with families and other learning environments to break down barriers to learning for children and young people.

Assistant educational psychologists also develop projects and services to improve educational provision. Pay for this role can vary and people can earn anywhere between £30,000 and £40,000 a year depending on the region and local authority.

ALTERNATIVE ROUTES AND DIFFERENT CAREER DIRECTIONS

If you feel like you don't want to pursue the educational psychology route and getting the educational psychology doctorate is too challenging or unappealing, there are plenty of ways to apply psychology to education. This can be through a role as a classroom teacher, a behavioural specialist, a researcher, an educational policy officer, a subject curriculum specialist or private tutor.

CASE STUDY

Dr Jason Apaloo-Shonibare, educational psychologist

Why educational psychology?

Using psychological theories to invest in the youth is one of the best ways they can be applied. Education and learning occupies so much of our lives that being trained to work at individual, group and broader systemic levels to support children and young people's development feels like such a privilege. The job can vary too, meaning special interests such as mine in critical research and different community practice models can be pursued. One thing I've always particularly appreciated about training to become an EP is the development of my reflective skills. With them I'm more attuned and better at problem-solving.

Advice to aspiring educational psychologists

I would always encourage anyone contemplating applying to train as an EP to speak with people actually doing the job. I found some invaluable insight for having done this ahead of getting on the professional doctorate. The course is a significant commitment which will undoubtedly require sacrifices. You'll need to be as sure as you can be about taking that step before you do. Thankfully we're a friendly bunch (mostly) so ask and hopefully someone will be able to give you some of their reflections post-qualification.

Dr Jason Apaloo-Shonibare's career timeline

Various Associate Roles | Educational Psychologist | Aug 2025–present

Hackney Education | Educational Psychologist | Sept 2021–Aug 2025 |

Tavistock and Portman NHS Trust | Educational Psychology Doctorate | Sept 2018–Sept 2021

The Michael Trippet School | EHCP and Outreach Leader | Feb 2017

Springboard Youth Academy | Safeguarding and Welfare Lead | June–Sept 2017

The Challenge | Programme leader | July–August 2017

Into University | Student Welfare Advisor | May 2015–Sept 2016

Kids Company | Assistant Psychologist and Team Leader in the Urban Academy | May 2012–May 2015

Kids Company | Therapeutic Key Worker in the Urban Academy | Jan 2012–May 2012

Camden and Islington NHS Trust | Senior Project Worker | Nov 2009–Nov 2011

British Psychological Society | Elected Committee Member | 2010–2012

Camden and Islington NHS Trust | Project Officer, Afro-Caribbean Mental Health Resource Centre | Dec 2008–Oct 2009

University of East London | BSc Psychology | 2005–2008

CHAPTER SUMMARY

- Educational psychologists often work with schools and educational institutions in local authorities in the UK to support the learning of children and young people.
- A career in educational psychology can be varied and interesting. To be a qualified educational psychologist, you would need to have a psychology undergraduate degree, followed by some work experience in teaching, teaching assistance or assistant educational psychology roles.
- Educational psychology doctorates are also government-funded in the UK by the Department for Education but receive less funding than the clinical psychology doctorate. If you do gain a place on the educational psychology doctorate, you won't need to pay tuition fees and will receive a small stipend.
- Skills that are paramount in this role include self-awareness, teamwork, relationship management, collaboration, report writing and attention to detail.

5

FORENSIC PSYCHOLOGY

WHAT IS FORENSIC PSYCHOLOGY?

This area applies psychological theory to criminal investigations and focuses on understanding the psychology of criminal behaviour. Forensic psychologists work with the treatment of those who have committed offences or crimes. Forensic psychologists work with offenders who have committed various crimes including sexual offences, aggression, violence and they also work with them to reduce drug and alcohol dependencies. Forensic psychologists work with those who deal with or are involved in the criminal justice system and often apply psychological methods to reduce the impact of criminal reoffending.

Forensic psychologists work with other professionals from different agencies including the police, probation services and prison services as well as young offender institutes. Forensic psychologists work on a variety of projects and pilot and implement treatment programmes to reduce reoffending, workshops to reduce stress for staff and prisoners, research to provide evidence for practice, prisoner profiling and they give expert evidence in courts and provide crime analysis.

DOI: 10.4324/9781003669449-6

Forensic psychologists also work with those who are at risk of offending, family members, victims and the public who are affected by crime. They can work and be employed by the NHS, private healthcare providers, specialist mental healthcare settings, social services, offender management services and in academic sectors.

WHAT QUALIFICATIONS DO I NEED TO BE A FORENSIC PSYCHOLOGIST?

Those who would like to pursue this area of psychology need to complete an undergraduate psychology degree accredited by the British Psychological Society (BPS). The next step is to complete an accredited master's degree in forensic psychology, which can be completed full-time in one year or two years or part-time. The modules covered on an accredited MSc programme include the treatment and assessment of offenders, risk assessment methods and treatment of offenders with mental health and personality disorders, legal and criminology concepts and social issues in organisations.

After completing a master's degree, the next step is to gain the stage 2 qualification in forensic psychology (QFP). This involves a minimum of two years supervised practice in different professional areas of forensic psychology. This is expected to be done at the same time as working as a trainee forensic psychologist. Some universities offer a route to complete a doctoral programme in forensic psychology, which can be done instead of the independent QFP route. The doctorate route offers the qualification in forensic psychology (QFP) and an additional research component, which is the doctoral thesis. Either the independent route or the forensic psychology doctorate can give you the practical component needed to be a qualified forensic psychologist.

TOP-UP DOCTORATES

Some universities offer a two-year top-up doctorate, which can be completed in two years and gives individuals the practical and doctoral elements of completing a research project or thesis. This can be done after the master's degree. This is offered by a limited number of universities but will allow you to have the qualification in forensic psychology needed to be a qualified psychologist.

WHAT WORK EXPERIENCE DO I NEED TO GET ONTO THE MSC FOR FORENSIC PSYCHOLOGY?

Having and gaining work experience is an important way to understand whether you want to pursue this area. Forensic psychology experience can be gained from working with victim support, witness services, working in hostels, refuges, drug and alcohol treatment centres, prisons, secure hospitals and rehabilitation units and young people's services such as youth offending services. Trainee forensic psychology roles are also available too.

Many forensic psychologists move into careers in the NHS, working as treatment leads for therapy and supporting forensic wards. Forensic psychology training routes are not funded by the government and thus master's and doctoral programmes either need to be self-funded or funded by scholarships. Roles you can do to increase your experience include an intervention facilitator or a trainee forensic psychologist. Intervention facilitators deliver interventions with the aim of leading to a reduction in offending. Facilitators deliver group sessions to prisoners.

SALARY

Forensic psychologists can be paid between £31,365 and £44,503 and more with more years of experience and further specialisms.

HOW DO I KNOW IF THIS ROUTE IS FOR ME?

If you are interested in working with offenders and want to understand criminal behaviours, have empathy, kindness, great communication skills, and can work well under pressure and in unpredictable environments, forensic psychology is for you.

WHAT'S THE REALITY?

You probably know what I am going to say, it's competitive, as with all the routes. However, as the professional doctoral route to becoming fully qualified is often self-funded, competition may be less than in the educational and clinical psychology routes. There are roles advertised for forensic psychologists, both trainees and other roles that can allow you to have the experience you can use to go down the QFP route.

ALTERNATIVE ROLES

If you feel like you don't want to pursue the full qualification and stop after the master's degree, you can still pursue roles in forensic psychology if you are still finding it hard to get an independent training place. This can be working as a prison or probation officer, working in youth offending or youth justice boards, a social researcher, a policy maker or a criminal intelligence analyst.

CASE STUDY

Dr Amber-Renee Gayle, forensic psychologist

Dr Amber-Renee Gayle is a qualified forensic psychologist, and she was enrolled on a top-up professional doctorate at the University of Nottingham, which she completed in 2021. Amber-Renee completed her undergraduate degree in Psychology from the University of Hertfordshire. After this degree, she worked as a mental health care assistant in Birmingham and supported women with long and enduring mental ill health in a community setting. She developed stakeholder management and listening, administration, safeguarding and team working skills.

Amber-Renee then completed her master's degree in forensic psychology at Birmingham City University in 2018. This master's served the 'stage 1' part of becoming a chartered forensic psychologist. Amber-Renee became an assistant psychologist in a West Midlands NHS trust where she previously volunteered. In this role, she specifically worked in a secure mental health setting with men who were high-risk and had presented with complex, long-term problems at risk of offending. After this, Amber-Renee completed a two-year doctoral top-up course, which enabled her to become a fully qualified forensic psychologist. The two-year top-up course is an alternative to a traditional three-year doctorate. During the two years, Amber-Renee had a variety of placements in secure units and at a private forensic psychology firm, which offered a variety of services, including expert court proceedings, therapeutic services, parole board assessments and assessments of psychological functioning. She is currently working at Northamptonshire Healthcare NHS Foundation and works as a registered forensic psychologist.

Why I chose forensic psychology

I enjoy applying psychology to a criminal justice setting and I feel my character and personality naturally lends itself to helping others. Most of the individual forensic psychologists work with are considered some of the most disliked in society due to offences they have committed. I understand this perception, and I also understand there are many layers to people who are part of the forensic population. History, biology, experiences, and core beliefs can really influence people. Exploring ways to engage people, supporting them to identify these factors and encouraging them really interested me. I see first-hand how I can empower them to live an offence-free life, which is rewarding for me and the service user.

One piece of advice for aspiring forensic psychologists?

Try and gain experience working in a forensic setting. This could be in a secure unit or secure hospital, with the prison service, probation, or a forensic community team. You don't necessarily need a job as an assistant psychologist in these settings, but roles such as support worker and health care assistant are equally valuable in understanding the context. I would also encourage those aiming to get a role in forensic psychology to find a mentor or speak to qualified forensic psychologists to help facilitate their understanding of the role and what it entails.

Dr Amber-Renee's career timeline

Registered Forensic Psychologist | Northampton Healthcare NHS Foundation | Aug 2023–present

Trainee Forensic Psychologist | Northampton Healthcare NHS Foundation | May 2021–June 2023

University of Nottingham | Professional Doctorate, Forensic Psychology (two-year top-up) | Sept 2019–July 2021

Placements: Forensic Psychology Practice & Brookland Secure Hospital, Birmingham and Solihull Mental Health Trust,

Assistant Psychologist | Sept 2018–Sept 2019

MSc Forensic Psychology | Birmingham City University | 2017–2018

Birmingham and Solihull Mental Health Trust | Volunteer | July 2017

Servol Community Trust | Mental Health Care Assistant | June 2015–Aug 2018

Teaching Assistant | Hamstead Hall Academy Trust (volunteer) | 2014–2015

Mentor | Aug 2013–2014

University of Hertfordshire | BSc Psychology | 2012–2015

CHAPTER SUMMARY

- This is a perfect area for you if you are interested in working within criminal justice settings including with perpetrators and victims of violence and harm.
- Unlike clinical and educational psychology, there are two routes to qualification in forensic psychology. After a master's degree, you can pursue a top-up doctorate or do the QFP qualification whilst working in a forensic setting, such as a prison.
- Forensic psychology is a non-funded route, which means that UK departments do not pay course fees as they do for clinical or educational psychology. Based on this, to go down the professional doctorate route, you'd have to self-fund either

the professional doctorate route or, when completing the QFP, independently.

- Even if you don't want to qualify as a full forensic psychologist, there are many roles you can do after an undergraduate degree in psychology or after a master's degree in forensic psychology, including drug and alcohol treatment centre worker, academic researcher in forensic populations, prison officer, probation officer, victim advocate or policy researcher.

6

COUNSELLING PSYCHOLOGY

Counselling psychology uses psychological theory and research to help clients with a range of life changes and mental health conditions. Clients can include children, adults, families, couples and groups and the work revolves around helping people to cope with anxiety, depression, bereavement, relationship difficulties and traumas. The mental health concerns that counselling psychologists help with include anxiety, depression, eating disorders, post-traumatic stress disorder (PTSD) or psychosis. Counselling psychologists work with people to allow them to become self-aware, take control or their recovery and consider change.

Counselling psychologists work in healthcare and forensic services like the National Health Service (NHS), prisons, probation services, private practice, research, consultancies and charities. Counselling psychologists to maintain their ability to practise engage in their own personal therapy and supervision too.

Counselling psychologists provide assessments of mental health needs, conduct risk assessments and administer and interpret psychometric assessments to better understand the clients they work with. Counselling psychologists also work collaboratively with clients based on respect and compassion and work as part of multidisciplinary teams with psychiatrists, occupational therapists, wellbeing practitioners, psychiatric nurses and social workers.

DOI: 10.4324/9781003669449-7

HOW CAN I BECOME A COUNSELLING PSYCHOLOGIST?

Individuals interested in pursuing counselling psychology must complete a British Psychological Society (BPS)–accredited undergraduate degree or a psychology conversion course if they have previously completed another degree. At the undergraduate level, they will need to have achieved a 2:1 grade or higher, evidence or a postgraduate degree to show research ability. Individuals then have two options, similar to forensic psychology. Either you complete a BPS-accredited doctorate in counselling psychology or complete the BPS stage two qualification in counselling psychology (QCOP). The QCOP is an independent route for becoming a qualified counselling psychologist.

To get a place on the independent route, you'll need to be working in a trainee role, which can be paid or voluntary and engage with a supervisor on the BPS register of applied psychology practice supervisors. To gain a place on a doctorate or professional qualification, a minimum of one year's relevant work experience is often needed. This can be in an assistant psychology role, psychology wellbeing practitioner, health support worker, or health care assistant work.

FUNDING FURTHER STUDY

The study routes for either the doctorate in counselling psychology or the QCOP is self-funded. Additionally, courses and qualifications require you to pay for your own personal therapy and sometimes supervision. There are counselling psychology assistant roles employers sometimes fund studies. Additionally, some scholarships or bursaries are available.

WHAT'S THE DIFFERENCE BETWEEN CLINICAL PSYCHOLOGISTS AND COUNSELLING PSYCHOLOGISTS?

The work that clinical and counselling psychologists can be very similar. They can work in the same settings and work with the same/similar clients. In practice, counselling psychologists work in the very same fields, jobs and roles, often in the UK's NHS or engage in counselling clients privately, outside the NHS.

Additionally, most clinical psychologists have their training funded by the NHS, whereas counselling psychology doctorates and training routes are self-funded or sponsored by an employer. Clinical psychology training focuses on delivering cognitive behavioural therapy and one other therapeutic modality, whereas counselling psychology training covers several other modalities, including person-centred and psychodynamic theories.

WHAT YOU WILL LEARN ON A COUNSELLING PSYCHOLOGY PROFESSIONAL DOCTORATE

Counselling psychology doctoral courses focus on students learning about different approaches to counselling psychology, such as psychodynamic, person-centred, cognitive, behavioural, as well as humanistic theories. Additionally, the doctorate also includes modules related to professional development, diversity, inclusion, cultural awareness, psychometrics, neurodiversity, anti-discrimination and supervision modules. There will also be a research thesis that needs to be produced by the end of the course, which centres on an original research idea and investigation within the counselling psychology realm.

Learning approaches and assessments will vary, but many use a combination of group and peer learning, case studies, practice placement competency evaluations, reading and analysis, literature reviews, role plays and practicums, supervised placements, reflective journals and traditional lectures and seminars.

HOW MUCH DO COUNSELLING PSYCHOLOGISTS GET PAID?

If completing QCOP and you have secured a trainee role, you can be paid on an NHS Band 6 wage, from £30,401 to £37,267. Once qualified, psychologists go to Band 7 from £37,267 to £43,722. Once going through the ranks, salaries can go up towards £80,000 plus.

HOW DO I KNOW IF THIS ROUTE IS FOR ME?

If you are interested in having a more rounded and holistic learning and training method and are empathic, a good communicator as well as being thoughtful and analytical this route is for you.

WHAT'S THE REALITY?

With this route into psychology, it may be difficult to secure a supervisor all the way through the QCOP independent training route. If this is the route you want to go down, try and gather as much experience as possible in therapeutic settings in counselling services and working in the NHS, secure units and other places where counselling psychology support may be needed. You may also be interested in pursuing a master's degree in counselling psychology to gain more knowledge and increase your chances of getting a professional doctorate. This can help but if it's supported with some practical experience that is also a great combination.

ALTERNATIVE ROLES

If you don't complete stage two of training (this could be down to not having access to funding a professional doctorate or the independent stage two route) you can always pursue a role as a psychological wellbeing practitioner. Psychological wellbeing practitioners are employed by the NHS and work with people with common mental health conditions. The training to become a psychological wellbeing practitioner is funded, and you get paid whilst you train for a year. Additionally, you can try roles like assistant psychologist jobs and even research roles.

You can also decide to become a psychotherapist and counsellor and complete a master's degree or postgraduate diploma or master's degree in this area instead of completing the counselling psychology doctorate or completing the stage two qualification. Postgraduate counselling or psychotherapy courses are often not funded and also give you a different focus than if you work and train as a counselling psychologist. Psychotherapists and psychological wellbeing practitioners can work privately with clients outside of the NHS also.

CASE STUDY

Dr Orinayo Onabanjo, chartered counselling psychologist

Dr Onabanjo is a chartered counselling psychologist, who currently works as a perinatal counselling psychologist. Dr Orinayo has been able to work with a diverse range or clients from different ethnic and cultural backgrounds, from children to older adults. Dr Orinayo is also very interested working with people who have experienced perinatal mental health difficulties. Dr Onabanjo also delivers presentations workshops and talks on attachment, mental wealth, perinatal mental health, childhood trauma and authenticity.

> I chose counselling psychology because it resonated with a natural desire in me to support others as they navigate their experiences of psychological distress. Even now, it is rare to find spaces or people who can truly embody the emotional safety that is needed to find the strength and the resources to work through these difficulties. The reality of this ignited a deep conviction within me to be one of the safe ones, to be a relational home for the emotional suffering that is so often carried in silence and in isolation.
>
> I would say make sure that the decision is one that originates from the heart. You really have to be humble and have the genuine capacity and willingness to bear witness to the depths of another person's emotional suffering and not look away. For me that is the core of being able to do the job well.

Dr Orinayo's career timeline

Perinatal Counselling Psychologist | Hertfordshire Partnership University NHS Foundation Trust | Aug 2023–present

Founder | Black Aspiring Counselling Psychologists Forum | Nov 2020–present

Counselling psychologist | West London NHS Trust | Feb 2020–Aug 2023

Trainee counselling psychologist | NHS, Placement 4

Trainee counselling psychologist | One in 4, Placement 3

Trainee counselling psychologist | Place2be, Placement 2

Trainee counselling psychologist | Addiction, Placement 1

University of Surrey | Professional Doctorate in Counselling Psychology | 2015–2019

Women's Community Project Support Worker | Parents and Children Together | June 2014–Feb 2015

Student Intervention Worker | Cranbourne Business and Enterprise College | March 2013–March 2014

Counselling and Psychotherapy Training Academy | CPCAB Level 2 Certificate in Counselling Skills | 2013

Graduate Therapeutic Care Worker | The Walled Garden | Residential Community Care | Sept 2012–Oct 2012

University of Kent | BSc Psychology | 2009–2012

The Abbey School, Reading | A-levels, Drama, Psychology, History | 2007–2009

CHAPTER SUMMARY

- As with forensic psychology, counselling psychology professional doctorates are not funded by the NHS.
- To qualify as a counselling psychologist, you can either complete a professional doctorate in counselling psychology or do an independent route whilst working called the QCOP.
- Counselling psychologists can work in healthcare and forensic settings as well as privately and their training focuses heavily on other counselling theories and modalities such as person-centred, humanistic and psychodynamic as well as cognitive behavioural therapy.
- Counselling psychology offers both variety or specialism and can be flexible to the needs and careers of many people.

7

HEALTH PSYCHOLOGY

WHAT IS HEALTH PSYCHOLOGY?

Health psychologists apply psychological theory and knowledge to promote general wellbeing and health, and to understand the psychological impact of physical and psychological illness. Many health psychologists help individuals manage chronic illnesses and support their recover and they can help and encourage people to live healthier lives by promoting things like smoking cessation, weight loss and exercise.

Health psychologists can advise and train medical doctors on more effective ways to communicate with their patients. They can devise interventions to help increase healthy behaviour and encourage behaviour change and work with those who suffer from chronic pain to help them manage their pain. Additionally, health psychologists can also work with patients who have cancer, organ transplants, cardiac rehabilitation, strokes and diabetes. Health psychologists can help these individuals cope with and adapt to their new situations and realities during or after an illness.

Psychological theories such as cognitive-behavioural, self-esteem, locus of control and self-belief may be used by health psychologists to encourage healthier behaviours and lifestyles.

DOI: 10.4324/9781003669449-8

Health psychologists work in multidisciplinary teams, with doctors, nurses, health researchers, public health practitioners, dieticians and nutritionists.

WHERE DO HEALTH PSYCHOLOGISTS WORK?

Health psychologists can work in community settings such as local authorities, councils, hospitals, private healthcare providers such as Bupa or Axa. Also, health psychologists can work as academic researchers or lecturers in universities. Additionally, they can work independently as self-employed and contract or work on projects for different organisations.

HOW DO I BECOME A HEALTH PSYCHOLOGIST?

As with all psychology professions, having an undergraduate degree in psychology is a prerequisite, and one that is recognised by the British Psychological Society. After completing the undergraduate degree, the next step is to apply for postgraduate studies. Most universities will require a good qualification at undergraduate level, usually a 2:1, but a 2:2 with good work experience can also help you gain a place on a master's course in health psychology. After an accredited master's degree in health psychology, a person can work towards gaining the British Psychological Society's (BPS) qualification in health psychology (QHP) independently or complete a professional doctorate in health psychology.

To gain a place on the health psychology doctorate or to complete the stage two requirement independently, you will need to be employed in a health psychology-related role. There are some trainee health psychology roles; however, other roles that count include research roles, public health roles, sexual health advisors, health promotion and nutrition type roles, etc. For the independent route, you'll need to complete at least two years of full-time supervised practice. Both the first two years of the doctorate and the two years of the independent route, you will be covering certain competencies, including consultancy, professional practice, psychological interventions, research, teaching and training. The doctoral route is the same as the independent route for the first two years, but the doctoral aspect requires an independent research project.

WHAT WORK EXPERIENCE COUNTS?

If gaining a place on the health psychology master's degree or doctorate, getting related work experience can be invaluable. Experience can be voluntary or paid and can be gained through shadowing a health psychologist or can include conducting research into health psychology topics, working as a healthcare assistant, working in mental health services, local general practitioners (GPs) or clinics, or working in healthcare charities. Additionally, gaining experience in areas such as drug rehabilitation centres and clinics specialising in eating disorders can be a way to learn about aspects of health and psychology.

HOW DO I KNOW IF THIS ROUTE IS FOR ME?

This is the ideal area for you if you are interested in how psychology and health intersect and are related. If you are curious about improving health outcomes, enhancing them and ensuring that both health professionals and their patients receive the best possible outcomes, this route is for you.

HOW MUCH DO HEALTH PSYCHOLOGISTS GET PAID?

After qualifying, NHS salaries often start at Band 7, which is from £43,742 to £50,056 and this can rise to up to £96,000. This is a guide and doesn't mean every health psychologist would be at these kinds of salaries, especially if working outside of the NHS.

WHAT'S THE REALITY?

Getting a health psychology doctorate may be an option, as most programmes require you to be in a related role while on the course. As this is a self-funded route, consider your options and how important this is to you. You can still work in related roles at the same time as studying, even without the QHP or professional doctorate, where you can effectively apply psychology to health and wellbeing.

ALTERNATIVE ROLES

This is a less common area of psychology and as such roles with the title 'health psychologist' may be hard to come by, especially if you are looking for roles outside of the NHS. Other roles you can do which would count towards qualifying for the independent route (QHP) or instead of including public health officer, health researcher, sexual health worker, wellness expert, health and safety officer, wellbeing practitioner or smoking cessation worker.

CASE STUDY

Dr Uzochi Nwaosu, professional doctorate in health psychology

Dr Uzochi completed his professional doctorate in Health Psychology at the University of the West of England (UWE) in Bristol UK in 2022. Uzochi began his journey to psychology by completing an undergraduate degree in psychology at the University of Bedfordshire. Zoch first heard about this area of psychology at a young age and was determined and fascinated by this area of psychology early on.

> From a young age I was interested in understanding psychological influences on health behaviours. e.g. As a young person I was constantly told about the increased susceptibility to chlamydia among people of my age group but I couldn't understand why rates of condom use among young people were low. This is despite awareness about the implications of unprotected, condomless sex. Health psychology has provided me with an understanding of effective ways to affect health behaviours in a positive way. I found health psychology very relatable and applicable to many areas of my personal life, which made the concepts even easier to grasp.

Uzochi has specialised in sexual health and applies health psychology theories to encourage safer sexual practices and to spread awareness of conditions in marginalised communities.

Advice to aspiring health psychologists

> The discipline is relatively young and constantly evolving, growing and developing. It is broad too, which provides those who are interested with endless opportunities, which you may not necessarily be exposed to if training in other psychology disciplines. Also, don't hesitate to reach out to current trainees, I am a qualified health psychologist for health and information. I have found the health psychology community to be close and a supportive one where people are always willing to help.

Dr Uzochi Nwaosu's career timeline

NHS | Sexual Health Advisor | April 2020–present

Visiting Lecturer | New City College, Hackney | Jan 2019–April 2020

Consultant Trainer and Educator | Bright Prospects Consultancy | Feb 2018–present

University of the West of England | Doctorate in Health Psychology | 2018–2021

Compass-Safe East | Health and Wellbeing Practitioner | April 2018–April 2020

Development Worker | Shine | Dec 2018–March 2019

Development Worker | East London NHS Foundation Trust | Aug 2014–Nov 2017

Metro Charity Sexual Health | Outreach Worker | May 2012–Jan 2015

University of Bedfordshire | MSc Health Psychology (stage 1) | Dissertation-the impact of hormonal contraception on condom use and STI perceptions among young people 2013–2014

University of Bedfordshire | BSc Psychology (with a health psychology focus) | 2009–2012

CHAPTER SUMMARY

- Health psychologists help promote general wellbeing and health and try to understand the psychological impact of physical and psychological illness.
- Health psychologists create and develop interventions to increase healthy behaviour and encourage behaviour change.
- Health psychologists often work with those who suffer from chronic pain to help them manage their pain and new realities.
- This route is self-funded and to qualify as a health psychologist, you can either complete a professional doctorate after an accredited undergraduate degree in psychology and an accredited master's degree in health psychology or complete the independent route called QHP.

8

OCCUPATIONAL PSYCHOLOGY

WHAT IS OCCUPATIONAL PSYCHOLOGY?

Many people get confused about what this area of psychology is; it often gets mistaken for occupational therapy, which is a totally different discipline. Occupational psychology is the application of psychology to work and organisations. It is concerned with helping organisations get the best out of employees and centres on providing optimum environments for individuals to grow and thrive at work. As people spend a substantial amount of time at work over a lifetime, it's important that this time is worthwhile for both parties. Organisational psychology focuses on workplace behaviour and aims to increase motivation, job satisfaction and overall organisational effectiveness.

Occupational psychology is also known as organisational, industrial, business and work psychology. These psychologists are concerned with five areas, which include:

1. Learning, training and development.
2. Leadership, engagement and motivation.
3. Wellbeing at work.
4. Work design, organisational change and development.
5. Psychological assessment at work.

DOI: 10.4324/9781003669449-9

Organisational psychologists apply theory and evidence-based practice to lots of different workplace projects. These projects include organisational change processes, the design of selection and assessment campaigns, psychometric assessments for recruitment and the development of wellbeing strategies. By working as an occupational psychologist, you can support and collaborate with human resource practitioners, ergonomists and human factors specialists, coaches and careers advisors.

The work of an occupational psychologist can vary widely and depends heavily on the work setting they find themselves in. Many occupational psychologists don't have job titles as 'occupational psychologists' and they often find roles in management consultancies, coaching and outsourcing companies, recruitment agencies, as HR professionals' trainers and independent consultants. Occupational psychologists also work in public-sector government bodies such as the Home Office, the Ministry of Justice and the Ministry of Defence. Occupational psychologists can also work in private sector organisations, including consultancies, psychometric test publishers and increasingly start-up or digital technology companies.

WHAT QUALIFICATIONS DO I NEED TO BE AN OCCUPATIONAL PSYCHOLOGIST?

As with all psychology professions an undergraduate degree is needed that is accredited by the British Psychological Society (BPS). After the undergraduate degree, completing a MSc/master's degree that is also accredited by the BPS, taking one year full-time or two years part-time. Getting onto a master's course can be easier if you have relevant work experience, e.g., voluntary or paid. This can be in recruitment roles, learning and development administration or HR administration. After the master's degree completing the stage two BPS qualification in occupational psychology (QOP) which consists of a minimum of two years full-time or equivalent supervised practice. To do this, you'll need to be employed as a trainee occupational psychologist or in a role related to occupational psychology, and you will gain support from a supervisor. There is also a doctorate in occupational psychology offered at one university in the UK, where the first two years are the same as the independent route and the final year is focussed on a doctoral thesis.

Gaining the qualification in occupational psychology and becoming a chartered occupational psychologist is something that is quite difficult. As highlighted earlier, finding roles called 'trainee occupational psychologist' aren't common and the self-funded independent route can be quite expensive. Those who have completed master's degree in occupational psychology can still work in occupational psychology roles and settings and can also work in associated roles, e.g., HR, coaching, training, academia research or recruitment and actively work to apply psychology to the workplace.

HOW DO I KNOW IF THIS ROUTE IS FOR ME?

If you enjoy and are interested in how psychology can be applied to the world of work, are fascinated by getting the best out of people in work settings, are great at communication, influencing and problem-solving this area and specialism is for you.

WHAT'S THE REALITY?

This route in terms of getting onto a MSc after graduation to fulfil the stage one, isn't as competitive as other areas of psychology. If you demonstrate interest in the area and have some evidence of relevant work experience you will be able to study at a postgraduate level.

However, what is difficult is completing the stage two (QOP) part. There are very few roles and that you can find that may sponsor you to become a chartered occupational psychologist if you want to go down the independent route. Some do occur in the civil service and others in private consultancies, but they aren't common.

HOW MUCH DO OCCUPATIONAL PSYCHOLOGISTS GET PAID?

Occupational psychologists' salaries vary and can range from £27,000 postgraduation to over £70,000 at senior consultant levels. As occupational psychologists work in both private and public-sector organisations, this can account for the variation in salaries.

ALTERNATIVE ROLES

Experiences and roles that may count or you can work in without being chartered and still apply psychology to the world of work include career and executive coach, workplace wellbeing practitioner, HR business partner, HR advisor, recruiter, trainer, human factors specialist, lecturer in HR, business or organisational psychology, researcher and health and safety advisor.

CASE STUDY

Winnie Frimpong, organisational psychologist

Winnie is a business psychologist working currently for small consultancy. She specialises in training people on the use of psychometric assessments to use for selection, assessment and development purposes. She works with many different organisations. Before she got this role, Winnie worked with children and has a passion for developing and working with young people so they can feel confident in educational settings.

Why occupational psychology?

I have always been fascinated by human behaviour and in general how the human brain has evolved to understand and interact with our environment the way we have. I remember being known as a great listener and someone who provided great counsel to my nursery and primary school 'clients' who had very pertinent and sometimes existential queries about life that needed sound dissecting.

Of course, I did not know you needed a licence to practise that kind of psychology but I must say I was a pretty successful trainee psychologist! Following this keen interest in human behaviour and a critical life-changing moment in my life, I knew that I had to study psychology and hopefully become a clinical psychologist with a fancy couch in a fancy office.

Unfortunately, as I completed my undergraduate degree, I was certain that the clinical pathway was not what I had imagined it to be. I had a brief stint in a mental health trust as part of my placement and realised I wouldn't be a good fit for the work required and vice versa the working environment would have possibly been toxic for me as an individual. I also worked closely with educational psychologists when I worked as a teaching assistant in two primary schools and came to same conclusion as I did with clinical psychology.

After graduating, with no idea of how to use my psychology degree, I went into private education and worked as a manager of a tuition centre for two years. During that period, I was further exposed to another facet of psychology which I hadn't considered – psychology at work. It was apparent to me that there were various aspects of my work that would have benefitted from an objective or evidence-based approach.

We spend majority of our lives working and might need to see a clinical psychologist or a therapist due to the interplay between work-related stressors and personal stressors. I also read those occupational psychologists were among the higher earners within the field… I needed no further convincing.

Advice for aspiring occupational psychologists

> For aspiring psychologists, especially from minority backgrounds, I would recommend you network extensively to increase your social capital. Connect strategically with people on LinkedIn, join groups or associations that you may be interested in. Ask to be connected with people etc. No one's trajectory is linear however, knowing a person or two and seizing opportunities is a great way to frame your mindset around this journey.

Frame your work experiences to show transferrable skills such as communication and interpersonal skills. Roles in HR, Administration, Research are all great starting points especially if you specifically want to be a Chartered Psychologist. During your MSc be proactive in connecting with professors and course mates who might already have businesses or a widely networked. Start looking for roles before you start your dissertation. This might give you an idea of the direction you might want to take and the skillset needed. A great book to get is "How to become an Occupational Psychologist". It breaks down the various questions you might have in an accessible and succinct manner.

Winnie Frimpong – career timeline

Freelance Consultant | 2024–present

Culture Amp | Lead People Scientist | Aug 2021–2024

Managing consultant | Aston Business Assessments | Jan 2018–Aug 2021

Business consultant | Lovely Notebooks | March 2016–2017

University of Surrey | MSc Occupational Psychology | 2016–2017

Assistant Manager | Explore Learning | Aug 2014–Aug 2016

Residence Senior Mentor | Brunel University | Sept 2012–May 2013

Assistant Director | The Learning Centre | Jan 2013–Aug 2014

Teaching Assistant (Placement Year) | North Primary School | 2011–2012

Brunel University | BSc Psychology | 2010–2014

CHAPTER SUMMARY

- Occupational psychology is concerned with how people perform at work, such as how people are selected and assessed, how people are promoted, trained and also concerns how systems and organisational processes affect employees.
- Occupational psychologists are also called industrial, organisational, business and work psychologists.

- Occupational psychologists can work in several settings including private and public-sector organisations as well as charities in roles such as training, learning, development, executive coaching, people and human resources departments.
- To qualify as an occupational psychologist, you can either do a professional doctorate or independently complete a QOP professional qualification whilst working.
- Occupational psychology is a perfect route for you if you would like to apply psychology to business and organisations.

9

SPORTS AND EXERCISE PSYCHOLOGY

WHAT IS A SPORTS AND EXERCISE PSYCHOLOGIST?

Sports and exercise psychologists are concerned with optimising athletes' performance in their sports. Sports and exercise psychologists work with individuals, teams and organisations involved in sports and exercise. Some specialise in sport psychology and work with athletes and teams from the amateur to elite professional level, helping them deal and cope with the psychological aspects of sport. This also includes personal development and the enhancement of performance. Contrastingly, exercise psychologists work with the public to increase motivation and participation in exercise and encourage healthy lifestyles.

Sports and exercise psychologists assess clients' needs, abilities and behaviours, help people implement strategies to overcome difficulties and realise potential, and work with general practitioners (GPs), nutritionists, coaches and physiotherapists. You can also deliver workshops including topics such as mindfulness and goal setting. Additionally, you can research and apply these findings too.

DOI: 10.4324/9781003669449-10

HOW DO I BECOME A SPORTS AND EXERCISE PSYCHOLOGIST?

Undertaking an accredited undergraduate degree in psychology followed by an accredited master's degree in sports and exercise psychology are the initial steps to becoming a sports and exercise psychologist. After this, you complete stage 2 of the BPS qualification (QSEP) with a minimum of two years of supervised on-the-job training or by completing a professional doctorate. This is the same as forensic, counselling, health and occupational psychology routes.

WHAT WORK EXPERIENCE CAN I GET TO HELP ME GET ONTO THE MSC?

You can do this through paid work, volunteering or shadowing. Some people contact local sports clubs or leisure centres to gain experience, and this could be in personal training, health promotion or even teaching physical education (PE), many sports psychologists work in private consultancies or work for professional sports teams or national governing bodies. Many sports and exercise psychologists work within academia or research and combine private work with academia.

HOW DO I KNOW IF THIS ROUTE IS FOR ME?

If you are interested in applying psychology to the world of sports to optimise performance and self-belief in athletes and the general public, this route is for you. You may be an athlete or interested in sports yourself; you would need skills in communication, empathy, strategy and forward thinking, problem-solving, and working under pressure.

ALTERNATIVE ROUTES TO QUALIFY AS A SPORTS AND EXERCISE PSYCHOLOGIST

CASES

The chartered association of sports and exercise sciences (CASES) is another qualification route some sports and exercise psychologists can choose to pursue alongside the British psychological society (BPS) route. The CASES division of sports psychology focuses on

Performance Excellence: processes and populations relating to human performance and enhancement.

Engagement and Development: factors, processes and stakeholders related to athlete development and sports and exercise participation.

Mental Health: factors and interactions related to mental health in a sports and exercise setting.

QUALIFICATION IN SPORTS AND EXERCISE PSYCHOLOGY ACCREDITATION ROUTE (SEPAR)

Application requirements

1. Underpinning psychology knowledge (e.g., an undergraduate degree)
2. MSc in sports and exercise psychology
3. A psychology conversion course (MSc) (if undergrad in an accredited course hasn't been done)

The SEPAR programme lasts anything between two and four years and you must have a minimum of 3,200 hours of practice and 20 hours of this needs to be observed by a supervisor. You will also need to submit a portfolio and go to core workshops.

WHAT'S THE REALITY?

Becoming a sports and exercise psychologist can be difficult; however, if you work in the area already, then you can apply this knowledge too; getting on the QSEP qualification route independently might be a more realistic prospect for you. Alternatively, you can qualify using the chartered association of sports and exercise sciences (CASES). Having relevant practical and research experience will help you complete the qualification independently or through the professional doctorate in sports and exercise psychology. It's also hard to get direct sports psychology experience due to client confidentiality. However, you may be able to attend workshops delivered by sports psychologists, participate in conferences and network.

HOW MUCH DO SPORTS AND EXERCISE PSYCHOLOGISTS GET PAID?

This can vary between £20,000–60,000 depending on your seniority and experience.

ALTERNATIVE ROLES

You can work in roles adjacent to sports psychology and still apply psychology to sports and exercise further study. These roles include fitness instructor, sports coach, salesperson, scout, PE teacher, researcher or academic who researches or specialises in sports and exercise psychology.

CASE STUDY

Dr Dawn-Marie Armstrong, sports and exercise psychologist

Dr Dawn-Marie is currently a qualified sports and exercise psychologist who completed professional doctorate at Liverpool John Moores university. Her career journey is extremely interesting. Dawn-Marie began her journey by completing her undergraduate degree in psychology from The Cave Hill campus of the University or the West Indies, in Barbados. Dawn-Marie also played amateur cricket for many years. Based on Dawn-Marie's interest in both sport and psychology, it was a lecturer who notified her of pursuing a career in sports and exercise psychology. After completing her undergraduate degree in psychology, Dawn-Marie then completed her stage 1 requirement to become a chartered sports and exercise psychologist at Northumbria in an MSc in sports and exercise psychology. After this, Dawn-Marie went back to Barbados and became a PE teacher in primary schools and then became a mental skills coach for Cricket West Indies under 19 World Cup squad. Dawn Marie then began her professional doctorate back in the UK in sports and exercise psychology at Liverpool John Moores university.

As part of Dawn-Marie's professional doctorate, has had placements as an Academy Psychologist at Fulham football squads' foundation phase for children aged 9–12 years old. During this placement she delivered mental skills training through engagement, psyche education and empowerment.

Dawn-Marie then became a sports psychology support at cricket Scotland where she worked with those on the talent development pathway with boys aged under 17 and 19. The team subsequently qualified for the ICC 2020 under 19 World Cup. Dawn-Marie is now in the final stages or completing her professional doctorate is working on her thesis and research project.

Why sports and exercise psychology?

> I chose Sports and Exercise Psychology as a career because being a former athlete myself, I saw the importance for mental preparation for optimal performance not just inside the arena but outside as well. I wanted to make an impact and facilitate change in the lives of those I was destined to work with. Seeing people become better versions of themselves always gave me great joy and I was keen to welcome the challenge of providing individualised service and support.

What advice would you give aspiring sports and exercise psychologists?

> Be yourself even though the world may try to dictate who you're supposed to be and how you practice. Always remember that you are at the centre of what you do. Your clients will appreciate it and it will make your work more enjoyable. Stand out and show the world who you are.

Dr Dawn-Marie's career timeline

Deans Associate Fellow | Loughborough University | Nov 2023–present

HE Lecturer Sport Psychologist | Loughborough College | Sept 2022–June 2023

DML Sports Psych | Freelance Consultancy delivering mental health skills training programmes across all teams sports and providing consultancy | Jun 2012–present

PSYPAG | Division of Sports and Exercise Psychology Representative | Aug 2018–July 2020

University of Stirling | Academic Tutor for MSc Sports Psychology | Feb 2020–June 2020

Sports Psychology Support | Cricket Scotland | March 2018–March 2020 (Placement for Professional Doctorate)

Academy Psychologist | Fulham football club, Placement for Professional Doctorate | Nov 2018–June 2019

Professional Doctorate in Sports and Exercise Psychology | Liverpool John Moores University | 2018–2021

Mental Skills Coach | Cricket West Indies | Aug 2015–Jan 2018

PE Teacher, The Lester Vaughn school, Barbados | Sept 2014–Oct 2017

Northumbria University | MSc Sports and Exercise Psychology | 2011–2012

The University of the West Indies | BSc Psychology | 2006–2010

CHAPTER SUMMARY

- Sports and exercise psychologists work with athletes and the general population and aim to optimise performance and increase exercise behaviours.
- Sports and exercise psychologists can either focus on the sports or exercise side or do a combination of both. They can also work with elite sports teams and athletes or with

local communities to increase exercise behaviours and sports self-efficacy.

- To qualify as a sports and exercise psychologist, there are about three options. With the British psychological society, you can complete a professional doctorate in sports and exercise psychology after an accredited undergraduate and Master's degree or you can do the independent route, QSEP.
- Another route you can go down is to do a CASES qualification from the chartered association of sports and exercise sciences and complete a qualification in sports and exercise psychology accreditation route (SEPAR).
- This applied area is great if you are interested in how to help people increase their performance in sports or exercise settings.

10

ACADEMIC PSYCHOLOGY

One area we haven't highlighted in this book is a career area of psychology that many people often overlook. This area is for those who want to have an academic career or a teaching career in psychology. Some people may start off with a career in applied psychology, such as clinical, counselling, occupational, health or forensic psychology and then later in their careers may switch to a teaching and academic career. Academic psychologists usually work within universities or research institutions. They work to teach undergraduate, postgraduate and doctoral students. Additionally, academics also conduct research within the field of psychology.

Some research areas academic psychologists can investigate include:

- How human behaviour impacts health and health outcomes.
- The relationship between health and work in paid and unpaid adult social care workers.
- Investigating how the developing brain learns to process visual information and use it for efficient action, perception, and decision-making.

DOI: 10.4324/9781003669449-11

- Investigating the role of sleep and circadian disruption in mood disorders and their comorbidity with cardiometabolic disease.
- Recruiting 300 newly diagnosed people with dementia from Black, South Asian, Caribbean and other minority groups as well as 150 people with dementia who identify as LGBTQ+.

HOW DO I BECOME AN ACADEMIC PSYCHOLOGIST?

You will need to have completed an undergraduate degree in psychology that has graduate basis for chartered membership (GBC). You would mostly need to then complete a Master's degree in an area of applied psychology that you are interested in or a research master's. It is possible to get a university teaching post with a master's degree but many lecturing positions do require a PhD. The PhD can be on any topic related to psychology, including neuropsychology, occupational, developmental, clinical, counselling, sports and exercise, health or forensic psychology.

PhD topics can be varied and diverse and can include things such as:

- Examining the cognitive, emotional and social consequences of encephalitis occurring in childhood and how these consequences compare to those associated with other acquired brain injuries.
- Treating children and young people with eating disorders: demonstrating the viability of a brief, effective, accessible and scalable therapy.

FUNDING A PHD

As highlighted in separate chapter funding a PhD or a master's degree you can go through a few routes.

Funding for PhD studies usually comes from studentships. Studentships are funding structures to cover PhD fees and a living stipend. The funding comes from a combination of sources including research councils, charities and grants from the university that is offering them. Other funding routes include self-funding through accessing postgraduate student loans or working whilst studying and self-funding. More information on this can be found in the introduction chapter.

WHAT'S IT LIKE BEING AN ACADEMIC PSYCHOLOGIST?

Academic psychologists often teach and lecture to undergraduate and postgraduate students. This includes designing and leading modules, marking papers, supervising Master's and PhD students' theses, conducting research, staff training and lecturing. The role is varied and requires planning, organisation, teamwork, critical thinking and programme management to name but a few skills.

HOW DO I KNOW IF THIS ROUTE IS FOR ME?

If you have a passion for researching different areas of psychology and you are also interested in teaching and creating unique learning environments, this route is for you. The route is varied and different, allowing for a kind of portfolio career. A lot of academic psychologists are also practitioner psychologists too and combine their academic work with freelance or consultancy work.

SKILLS YOU WILL NEED

To be an academic psychologist, you will need verbal and written communication skills, planning and organisational, project management, numeracy, stakeholder management and comprehension skills.

HOW MUCH DO ACADEMIC PSYCHOLOGISTS GET PAID?

Academic psychologists earn between £41,000 and £60,000 per year. This can vary with experience and time in the role.

CASE STUDY

Dr Uracha Chatrakul Na Ayudhya, academic psychologist

Why I went into academia

Academia has been in my blueprint since childhood. For as long as I can remember, my parents have drummed into me that formal education is the greatest 'gift' they could pass on to my brother and me. My mother was the first person in her family to attend university and obtained a BSc in Biology from Chulalongkorn University, Thailand's oldest university. Over a decade later, my father joined the same university as a senior lecturer after obtaining a PhD from the UK. Their commitment to formal education is one of the key reasons why my family left our home country, Thailand.

From the age of 14, I focused on studying psychology at university because I was interested in understanding human behaviour, so I could 'help' people. In my early 20s, I carried this intention with me as I specialised in organisational psychology for my MSc studies, believing I could help people at work achieve good working lives while, at the same time, helping organisations better support their workers to do their best work. My formal education has not taught me to see the extractive and exploitative capitalist labour relations that I was aiming to uphold.

I started my PhD with the same ambition to help workers and organisations, focusing on university students' sensemaking of 'work-life balance' before they complete their university education and enter the labour market as full-time workers. I was studying people like me who had worked casual jobs whilst studying at university and have yet to experience full-time work. In essence, I was studying myself – someone curious to understand what the world of work was like, without yet having fully experienced it.

Today, I have been a full-time academic for two decades. During this period, universities have changed due to the neoliberalisation of academia and feels almost irreversible and irreparable, with damaging consequences for the sector's workers and students. Why I came into academia no longer resonates and differs to why I remain.

Throughout all of this, I continue to learn from my experience as an educator, researcher, thinker and writer, working as an insider/outsider within organisational psychology as a subject discipline.

Most of all, I learn from and with my colleagues and my students about how to collectively and critically take notice, question, call out, resist, reimagine and above all else, take action against pedagogy, knowledge and practices that normalise and promote imperialist and colonialist logics of domination, oppression and dehumanisation. Organisational psychology as a subject discipline cannot be exempt from this (case in point: the unacknowledged colonialist, racist, eugenicist origins of modern-day psychometric testing). I remain in academia committed to working in community towards achieving liberation through education.

What advice would I give to aspiring academics?

Rather than imparting 'advice', please allow me to share my wish and hope instead. I wish for all aspiring academics to find meaningful communities, especially ones that provide space for members to collectively resist neoliberal logics of individualistic 'excellence', competition and 'survival of the fittest' in academia.

Dr Uracha Chatrakul Na Ayudhya's career timeline

Reader in Work and Organizations | Birkbeck, University of London | October 2024–present

Assistant Dean | Equalities and Diversity, School of Business, Economics and Informatics, Birkbeck, University of London | July 2020–August 2023

Senior Lecturer in Organizational Psychology | Birkbeck, University of London | October 2021–September 2024

Lecturer in Organizational Psychology | Birkbeck, University of London | February 2019–September 2021

Senior Lecturer | Organizational Behaviour and Human Resource Management, Middlesex University | September 2011–January 2019

Lecturer | Organizational Behaviour and Human Resource Management | Middlesex University | September 2007–August 2011

CHAPTER SUMMARY

- Academic psychologists mainly work within university and higher education settings but can also work within government institutions, think tanks or research consultancies.
- Academic psychologists can specialise in many areas of applied psychology such as cognitive, developmental, clinical, occupational and many other areas of psychology.
- Academic psychologists tend to need a PhD/professional doctorate or at least a master's degree in an applied area of psychology.
- Academic psychologists often work teach and lecture students, lead modules and collaborate with other academics for research purposes.
- This area is well-suited if you are interested in research and teaching psychological concepts and ideas.

11

INTERNATIONAL STUDENTS

According to a higher education statistics agency (HESA) report from 2022, international students accounted for 22% of the total student population in 2020/2021. The UK was the third most popular study destination for international students in 2019 (UNESCO Institute for Statistics, 2021), behind the USA and Australia. Chinese, Indian and Nigerian nationals were the top three nationalities among international students, according to a 2021 Universities UK study.

A HESA student record report from 2020/2021 found that 9,805 international students were studying psychology at the undergraduate level and 4,375 at the postgraduate level. Coming to the UK to study as an international student can be very challenging, as you have to juggle your studies as well as settling into a new country socially and academically.

UNDERGRADUATE

Those coming to the UK to study an undergraduate degree in psychology need to be aware of the entry requirements for their country. Also, it's important to check if your course has graduate basis for chartered membership (GBC), which allows you

DOI: 10.4324/9781003669449-12

to progress to postgraduate study in the UK as an applied psychologist. It is also important to research whether a psychology undergraduate degree in the UK is recognised in the country you want to return to/may want to return to.

POSTGRADUATE

Those who come to the UK as international students to study a master's, a PhD or a professional doctorate also need to check their eligibility to do these courses based on where they studied their undergraduate degrees. If international students wish to return to their home countries to practise after studying in the UK, it is crucial to verify whether the courses in the UK are recognised by their home country. If a student wants to practise in the UK as an applied psychologist, the postgraduate pathway should include them having GBC. This information can be found on the university's admission pages or through admissions departments.

FEES

For international students in the UK, there is no cap on fees across universities like there is for home students. Typically, undergraduate fees for psychology courses can range from £15,000 to over £40,000 a year. These fees do not include living costs, visa fees or immigration health surcharge.

For postgraduate courses, fees for master's degrees can be anything from £16,000 to £40,000 for full-time MSc courses. For PhD courses the fees can be anywhere from £17,000 to £35,000 per year for full time study. For professional doctorates, such as clinical psychology or educational psychology, the cost can be anything from £24,000 to £36,000 per year. It is to be noted that there are often a lot less places for international students on professional doctorates so getting a place on them may be very competitive.

GETTING INTERNATIONAL WORK EXPERIENCE

If you are thinking of pursuing a career in psychology and you haven't yet moved to the UK to study, try and get paid or voluntary experience in your home country. This can be within mental health services, hospitals, sports teams and gyms, consultancies, schools, recruitment agencies or prisons. These roles will provide you with experiences and roles that are aligned to many of the applied psychology routes.

CHAPTER SUMMARY

- This area discusses what to think about when choosing a psychology degree as an international student who wants to study in the UK.
- It goes over international student fees and what to think of if you want to practice in the UK or go abroad after studying in the UK.
- Lastly, the chapter covers how to find work experience as an international student.

12

CAREER DECISION MAKING – HOW DO DECIDE WHAT I WANT TO DO?

CAREER DECISION-MAKING THEORIES

Holland's RIASEC career theory

This theory was developed by John L. Holland (1959, 1997)[1] and his ideas were that people are matched to their careers and jobs based on their preferences and personality. Holland highlighted that there are six vocational personalities. This theory helps people think about their interests and how they relate to different roles and professions. These six areas include these areas: realistic, investigative, artistic, social, enterprising and conventional (RIASEC).

1. **Realistic** – people who like working more practically, with their hands, tools and machines and enjoys working outside and physical activity.

   Example careers include: mechanics, construction workers, electricians or farmers.
2. **Investigative** – people who enjoy observing, investigating, curious, analysing and solving complicated problems.

   Example careers include: researchers, medical doctors, scientists and computer programmers.

DOI: 10.4324/9781003669449-13

3. **Artistic** – those who prefer creative self-expression, people who value imagination and aesthetics.

   Example careers include: musician, actor, artist, author.
4. **Social** – those who like helping, instructing and working with others, these people tend to be empathetic and they enjoy teamwork.

   Example careers include: teacher, nurse, psychologist, social worker.
5. **Enterprising** – those who like to influence and lead others with good ideas with confidence.

   Example careers include: business owner, leader or senior manager.
6. **Conventional** – prefers traditional, structured and systematic work and environments, they are usually detail-oriented as well.

   Example careers include: administrator, data analyst, accountant or office manager.

This theory has a questionnaire associated with it and the area most related to psychology is the social category. As noted earlier, the most important factor in this theory is person-environment fit; however, this model has limitations. One of the limitations of the model is that it doesn't account for external factors such as economic, social, environmental or other factors that may impede career decision-making.

Additionally, for some, the theory doesn't adequately include how complex careers are and how they change over time. Also, the validity of the measure (does it measure what it should be measuring?), according to research, is quite weak.

For a psychology student or someone who is interested in psychology, the social category would be the most related career group. The categories are quite binary, but there can be examples of people having more than one career driver or more than one category (Warr, 2002).[2]

Nevertheless, the model is a good way for you to help decide which career direction a person should go into. Using this in combination with other methods may help you to be able to make career choices.

Another career theory we can talk about is Donald Super's developmental stage theory.

Questions

1. Apart from the social category, what other category would you identify with, if any?
2. How much do you need to fit into an organisation before you feel a part of it? Is that something you need to help you fit into an organisation?

SUPER'S LIFESPAN AND MODERN LIMITATIONS

Donald Super's theory of career development was created in 1953.[3] The theory emphasises that your career ideas and expression can change with time, and this is important when you plan your career.

1. **Growth – birth – 14**
   Development of self-concept or self-ideals, needs and the idea of work
2. **Exploration – 15–24**
   Testing and trying things out through hobbies, classes and skill development
3. **Establishment – 25–44**
   Entry level, skill development, organisational knowledge and building a foundation through work experience
4. **Maintenance – 45–64**
   Adjustment to improve the position to obtain optimum satisfaction
5. **Disengagement – 65+**
   Reduced output and prepare for retirement

The most important aspect of this theory is understanding your own self-concept, your drivers and your beliefs, and this can guide your career choice and path. With relation to psychology careers, the career for a lot of people starts in the exploration phase; however, a lot of people can have a career transition or change at their establishment phase or maintenance.

One of the criticisms of this theory suggests that the linear progression of the model is not always relevant to some people; not everyone has a career that unfolds linearly. Also, this model doesn't initially highlight the existence and how the external environment plays a part in the establishment of a career. As the model is older, it also doesn't take into consideration of modern patterns of work such as the gig economy or portfolio working. Additionally, another criticism is that the research theories were based on were of white, male, middle-class career norms and these models don't reflect a lot of individuals' experiences (Hunt and Rhodes, 2021).[4]

Another criticism of this theory is that for a lot of people the idea of career disengagement or decline after the age of 65 isn't necessarily the case in the modern world of work.

Questions

1. What career stage reflects where you are chronologically?
2. Whatever career stage you are at, think about how you can leverage your current skills and create the career you want.

THE SOCIAL-COGNITIVE CAREER THEORY

The social-cognitive career theory tries to explain three areas of career development. These include describing how academic and career interests develop: how educational and career choices are made and how career and academic success are obtained. The theory is based on Albert Bandura's (1986) social cognitive theory.[5] This theory was developed by Lent, Brown and Hackett in 1994.[6] The components of this theory include certain ideas, including self-efficacy beliefs, outcome expectations and personal goals.

SELF-EFFICACY BELIEFS

'What we believe we can do.' Self-efficacy beliefs are assumed to derive from our own experiences including accomplishments and vicarious experiences, social persuasion and physical and emotional states. Personal accomplishments and the messages we receive about these things include which social models or reinforcing messages people are exposed to. This can therefore affect a person's self-efficacy or confidence they have in themselves to achieve or do something.

OUTCOME EXPECTATIONS

'What we believe we believe will happen if we do it.' Outcome expectations are the beliefs people have about consequences or outcomes of completing behaviours, e.g., (if I do this, what will happen?). People are more likely to engage in behaviours that they think will be valued or lead to positive outcomes (e.g., high social standing, attractive work conditions, self-approval). Both self-efficacy and outcome expectations mediate an individual's efforts.

PERSONAL GOALS

'What we decide to do as a result.' Personal goals are separated into choice and performance goals. Personal goals suggest that people will be more likely to set goals they think are attainable and achievable. These goals tend to be related to career self-efficacy and outcome expectations. This also means that individual success or failure in something may help them to confirm or deny self-efficacy and outcome expectations.

This theory highlights that career development is a dynamic process which considers personal characteristics and attributes such as gender, ethnicity and age; learning experiences that shape self-efficacy and environmental supports or barriers which can either help or hinder outcomes. When it comes to this theory, it takes into consideration external and internal factors, as in an updated paper, Lent highlighted that these components are interrelated with these factors.[7]

For psychology students, this model can be very helpful in creating a framework to explore and maintain careers in psychology.

Firstly, psychology career self-efficacy can be developed by building up your confidence in your psychology knowledge. This can be done by keeping up to date with contemporary or past psychology theory, applying your knowledge via work experience in mental health and other organisational settings and learning and understanding the real experiences of those who are in a career you are interested in. Psychology career self-efficacy is about building up confidence in one's ability to perform in the study as well as in the end career. This can be explored by building up a bank of experiences in different areas of applied psychology or related careers.

Secondly, outcome expectations can be moderated by aiming for and preparing for positive outcomes when it comes to a psychology career. This involves alignment of and understanding of the career areas you as a psychology student, are interested in and then creating a positive idea of how you can achieve it. This could be from contacting your university or school careers service or finding a career coach or mentor to help you build up your career plan.

Thirdly, personal goals relate highly to outcome expectations and what will happen. So, writing specific and achievable goals that can be regularly checked, measured or monitored.

Questions

1. How can you build up your career self-efficacy in psychological careers?
2. How can you get more experience and advice in the field of psychological careers?
3. What top three goals to do you want to achieve in your career planning in the next few months?

INTELLIGENT CAREER THEORY

The intelligent career theory was developed by Arthur, Claman and DeFillippi (1995)[8] and highlights three areas to help you develop your career. This theory was developed at the time based on the rapid environmental changes in jobs in the mid-90s, including downsizing and outsourcing of a lot of functions.

Knowing why – what is your motivation for working or wanting to pursue a career in psychology?

Knowing how – what unique set of skills, knowledge, expertise or lived experience do you think you can bring to any job?

Knowing whom – how can you create, develop and maintain relationships with people you may need to help you develop your career?

Questions

1. Think about different careers you are interested in and why you are motivated to have those careers?
2. What top three skills do you think you have that can help an organisation or help you in your career?
3. How can you start to develop a network of people who can help and build your career?

KALEIDOSCOPE CAREER THEORY

This theory was developed by Maniero and Sullivan in 2005,[9] and they created it to demonstrate how careers change through a person's life. The three main components of this model include what they call the ABC of careers. The theory has been exposed as one that takes into account external factors.

Authenticity – your role and your work should match with your values, drivers and key skills.

Balance – emphasises work-life balance but also balance across all aspects of life.

Challenge – working life needs to be challenging and stimulating giving you the level of progression or career maintenance you need.

Questions

1. What are your core values and how does this affect the work you want to do?
2. How important is work-life balance to you and your career?
3. How important is to have a level of challenge or stimulation to the work you want to do?

PSYCHOLOGY CAREER QUIZ

Below is a psychology careers quiz and this could help you to think about which area of applied psychology you would like to specialise in.

1. **Which out of these options appeals the most?**
   a. I am interested in understanding people's drivers and understanding their mental health.
   b. I am interested in working with and understanding why people are drawn to crime and want to support the rehabilitation of those who are in the criminal justice system.
   c. I am interested in supporting children and young people to help them be the best they can be in their education.
   d. I am interested in working with people to help support with the link between their physical health and psychological health.
   e. I am interested in working to support athletes and members of the public with sport and exercise.
   f. I am interested in working with employees or organisations to create more optimum experiences for employees.
   g. I am interested in researching, teaching and supporting learners in psychological education.
2. **Which environment would you prefer to work in?**
   a. I am interested in working in health services, private and public to improve mental health.
   b. I am interested in working in prisons, forensic hospitals or young offenders' institutions.
   c. I am interested in working in schools, colleges or higher education institutions.
   d. I am interested in working in local authorities, within doctors' surgeries and with people in the community to help people who have health concerns lead more fulfilling and pain-free lives.

e. I am interested in collaborating with sports teams, athletes and gym staff to promote exercise and help individuals become more elite athletes.
f. I am interested in working within organisations and working directly with employees.
g. I am interested in working within universities, research institutes or higher education organisations.

3. **Which activities seem the most appealing to you?**

   a. Working one-to-one or in groups with clients to help improve mental health and wellbeing.
   b. Conducting observations, risk assessments and specifically working within the criminal justice system.
   c. Working with children and young people to help support, diagnose and advise others on how to enhance learning, especially those who are struggling in education.
   d. Helping people manage illnesses, pain and disability and promote healthy habits and a healthy outlook on health and wellbeing.
   e. Coaching and motivating athletes and those who exercise to perform better.
   f. Conducting and interpreting psychometric assessments, analysing employee data, conducting training or learning interventions within workplaces.
   g. Designing or conducting empirical research or teaching people about psychology.

4. **What type of challenge excites you most?**

   a. Understanding and treating mental health conditions.
   b. Exploring why people commit crimes and helping them change.
   c. Supporting children's development and learning.
   d. Promoting healthier lifestyles and managing physical illness.
   e. Helping others build resilience and mental strength.
   f. Improving teams, systems and organisational effectiveness.

g. Developing psychological theory and research to influence policy or practice.

5. **What impact do you want to make?**

a. Improving mental health and emotional wellbeing.
b. Reducing offending and supporting safer communities.
c. Enhancing educational outcomes for children and young people.
d. Helping people live healthier, longer lives.
e. Supporting others to achieve excellence and confidence in sports or exercise.
f. Creating fairer, happier and more effective workplaces.
g. Contributing new insights to the field of psychology through research or teaching people about psychology.

Count how many times you selected each letter (a–g). The letter that you have chosen the most indicates which area of psychology you would most align to, if there are two that you have chosen that's also workable (Table 12.1).

1. This section will help you to think about yourself and your skills, values and interests to help you to assess yourself

Skills
What are your key skills?

1.
2.
3.
4.
5.

Interest
What are you interested in?

1.
2.
3.
4.
5.

Table 12.1 Scoring diagram for career quiz

Letter	*Area of psychology*	*Description*
More A's	Clinical or Counselling Psychology	Supporting people with mental health challenges e.g., depression or psychology within health care settings
More B's	Forensic Psychology	Working with young offenders, those within the criminal justice system to rehabilitate and reduce offending
More C's	Educational Psychology	Support children and young people overcome barriers to learning
More D's	Health Psychology	Promote healthy support systems for those with chronic illnesses or those with disabilities
More E's	Sports and Exercise Psychology	Working with athletes and those who want to exercise and enhancing wellbeing to create optimum results
More F's	Occupational Psychology	Working with employees and organisations to support and create inclusive and optimum workplace environments
More G's	Academic Psychology	Working with students to teach them about psychology as well as research and contributing to psychological knowledge

PERSONALITY

How would you rate your personality based on these questions?

1. How open are you to new experiences on a scale of 1–5 (1 being not open at all and 5 being very open)
2. How conscientious are you when you are working on a scale of 1–5 (1 being not conscientious at all and 5 being very Conscientious)

3. How extraverted are you on a scale of 1–5 (1 being very introverted and 5 being very extraverted)
4. How agreeable are you on a scale of 1–5 (1 being stubborn, untrusting, 5 being trusting, cooperative)
5. How resilient are you on a scale of 1–5 (1 anxious, fearful and 5 being very emotionally stable)

VALUES

1. **What are your values?** e.g., creativity, integrity, leadership, family, accountability, empathy, courage, growth, honesty, fun, reliability, achievement, happiness.
2. **What's the most important thing for you when seeking work?** e.g., money, flexibility, values alignment, prestige.
3. **At the end of your career, what would you want to be remembered for?** e.g., the way you made people feel, your achievements, your resilience, your output, other?

CHAPTER SUMMARY

- This chapter introduces career theories that help individuals understand how to choose and develop their careers.
- This chapter highlights theories including Holland's RIASEC Theory, Super's lifespan theory, intelligent kaleidoscope and socio-cognitive career theories.
- This chapter then goes into a quiz and then some questions to help individuals highlight area/s of psychology to specialise in, followed by some questions about personality, skills, values and interest.

NOTES

1 Holland, J. L. (1997). *Making vocational choices. A theory of vocational personalities and work environments* (3rd ed.). Psychological Assessment Resources; Holland, J. L. (1959). A theory of vocational choice. *Journal of Counseling Psychology*, 6(1), 35–45.
2 Warr, P. (Ed.). (2002). *Psychology at work* (5th ed., pp. 182–183). Penguin Press.

3 Super, D. E. (1953). A theory of vocational development. *American Psychologist*, 8(5), 185–190.
4 Hunt, A. N., & Rhodes, T. D. (2021). Expanding the life-span, life-space approach using critical race theory and intersectionality. *Journal of College Access*, 6(3), Article 8.
5 Bandura, A. (1986). *Social foundations of thought and action: A social cognitive theory*. Prentice Hall.
6 Lent, R. W., Brown, S. D., & Hackett, G. (1994). Toward a unifying social cognitive theory of career and academic interest, choice, and performance. *Journal of Vocational Behavior*, 45(1), 79–122.
7 Lent, R. W., & Brown, S. D. (2013). *Career self-management: A social cognitive perspective*. In S. D. Brown & R. W. Lent (Eds.), *Career development and counseling: Putting theory and research to work* (2nd ed., pp. 381–411). Wiley.
8 Arthur, M., Claman, P., & DeFillippi, R. (1995). Intelligent enterprise, intelligent careers. *Academy of Management Executive*, 9(4), 7–19.
9 Mainiero, L. A., & Sullivan, S. E. (2005). Kaleidoscope careers: An alternate explanation for the opt-out revolution. *The Academy of Management Executive*, 19(1), 106–123.

13

CAREER DEVELOPMENT AND FREQUENTLY ASKED QUESTIONS

WHAT CAN I EXPECT FROM AN UNDERGRADUATE PSYCHOLOGY DEGREE?

As highlighted in earlier chapters, psychology undergraduate degrees cover many interesting topics. You can pursue a BSc or a BA in psychology; the former focuses on empirical areas such as quantitative research methods, while the BA degrees focus on humanities and social aspects of human behaviour. During your first year, many courses will focus on fundamental areas of psychology and lay the foundation for your learning. The areas of focus may include the foundations of psychology and the history and theories of the subject. The first year will also introduce you to areas such as cognitive, biological, developmental and social psychology.

Second- and third-year students focus on deepening their understanding of these areas and the third year often includes a research project or dissertation. Also, during these years, you are likely to be able to choose elective modules (e.g., you have more choice about the modules you study), whereas this is less likely to be an option in the first year. You can expect a significant amount of essay and report writing, team projects and reading journals and book chapters.

DOI: 10.4324/9781003669449-14

CAN I JUST DO MY UNDERGRADUATE AND BECOME A PROFESSIONAL PSYCHOLOGIST?

Another question that many people have is whether they can become professional psychologists after completing an undergraduate degree or even a master's degree. The answer is no. The undergraduate degree in psychology provides you with the tools and the baseline information needed to understand psychology. Master's degrees help you to specialise in a particular area.

To become a professional applied psychologist, depending on which area you focus on, you need to complete either a master's degree and/or a professional doctorate (clinical psychology and educational psychology), or a master's degree and supervised practice or a professional doctorate (for forensic, counselling, occupational, health and sports and exercise psychology).

This means the time it takes to be a qualified psychologist is either

3 + 3 (three-year full-time undergraduate degree + three-year professional doctorate for clinical, counselling and educational psychology routes). This doesn't include work experience components.

3 + 1 + 3 (three-year undergraduate degree, one-year master's, three-year professional doctorate).

WHERE DO I START TO FIND WHICH AREA I WANT TO PURSUE?

Trying to find an area of psychology that fits you can feel quite daunting but looking at the above figure can help you to conclude and decide on what different areas you may want to pursue (Figure 13.1).

HOW DO I GAIN EXPERIENCE IN PSYCHOLOGY?

Experience in psychology careers may feel daunting, overwhelming and confusing or they can feel like a fun challenge. Work experience, whether paid or voluntary, can help you to decide which areas of psychology you are interested in, whilst providing you with ways to acquire, develop and refine skills.

Diagram 2 "How do I choose which area of psychology to pursue?" (Page 62)

I am interested in supporting children and young people in education. I want to focus on their learning, development and wellbeing.	I am interested in supporting working with people of all ages to assess and treat a range of mental health conditions and psychological distress.	I am interested in supporting research related to how people behave, their experiences of the world and how they function. I am interested in exploring people's social, economic, cultural and spiritual experiences.	I am interested in using psychological theory to apply to criminal investigations and to help with psychological problems related to criminal behaviour and working with people who have committed criminal offences.	I am interested in using psychological theory to promote health behaviours and wellbeing. I want to understand the emotional and psychological aspects of health and illness and promote healthy behaviours.	I am interested in using psychological theory and practice to understand and enhance the workplace. I am interested in enhancing employee wellbeing, productivity, effectiveness, motivation and job satisfaction.	I am interested in using psychological theory and practice to work with athletes, sports teams, and coaches to improve performance and well-being. I am interested in helping people prepare for competition and cope with stress and improve mental health.
Educational Psychology	**Clinical Psychology**	**Counselling Psychology**	**Forensic Psychology**	**Health Psychology**	**Occupational Psychology**	**Sports & Exercise Psychology**
Key Skills Communication, empathy, data interpretation, and teamwork	**Key Skills** Empathy, active listening, analytical thinking, and critical thinking	**Key Skills** Active listening, empathy, emotional intelligence, analysis	**Key Skills** Communication, critical thinking, analytical thinking, adaptability	**Key Skills** Communication, empathy, data analysis, critical thinking, teamwork	**Key Skills** Communication, data analysis, critical thinking, research, adaptability, teamwork	**Key Skills** Communication, flexibility, analysis, teamwork.

Figure 13.1 Decision Diagram to Help You Chose Which Area of Psychology to Pursue

For each area of psychology, different types of experience may be needed; however, if you want to get any role after university just to earn money, this experience counts towards any post-graduate route. Generic work experience provides individuals with an opportunity to develop essential skills, including planning, organisation, written and verbal communication, teamwork, customer service and project management.

For each area of psychology, here are some more specific job titles, organisations or roles you may want to pursue (Table 13.1).

These job titles are not exhaustive, but they give you a start to help you find careers and experience in your field.

Table 13.1 Job titles for each applied area of psychology

Area of psychology	*Job roles*
Forensic	Work in a pupil referral unit, paid/voluntary roles at a young offender's team, working in a role at HM Prison Service e.g., prison officers, working with victim support, alternative provision schools, a role at a youth justice board, being an independent custody visitor, police officers, probation officers
Clinical	Mental health care assistant, assistant psychology roles work in social services, work as a support worker, volunteer work experience for charities such as Mind, research experience such research assistant. You can also do courses to become a psychological wellbeing practitioner (PWP) or clinical associate psychologist (CAP). If you do PWP or CAP training, you have to be in those roles for two years before you apply to the Clinical Psychology Doctorate
Counselling	Women's Aid, Child Line, Assistant Psychologist roles, Experience with charities such as Mind, Papyrus, Shout, or the Samaritans

(*Continued*)

Table 13.1 (Continued)

Area of psychology	*Job roles*
	You can also do courses to become a psychological wellbeing practitioner (PWP) or clinical associate psychologist (CAP). If you do PWP or CAP training, you have to be in those roles for two years before you apply to the Clinical Psychology Doctorate
Educational	School teacher, teaching assistant, assistant educational psychologist, tutor, learning mentor, literacy mentor, residential childcare officer, nursery nurse
Sports and exercise	Physical education (PE) teacher, sports coach, personal trainer, fitness instructor, research assistant, assistant psychologist
Health	Sexual health worker, trainee health psychologist, health promotion worker, wellbeing support worker, smoking cessation worker, research assistant
Occupational/ organisational	Trainee occupational psychologist, learning and development officer, recruitment officer, human resources officer, wellbeing manager, organisational change manager, psychometrician, occupational psychologist, business psychologist, work psychologist

I WANT A JOB WHERE I CAN 'USE MY DEGREE'

Many people say they want a job where they can 'use their degree' when completing their undergraduate. The implication of this statement is that if someone doesn't have a job title with 'psychologist' in it, they are wasting their degrees. As psychology undergraduate degrees become increasingly popular, not everyone who completes them wants to or can pursue a career in psychology. Based on this, there are many roles, both associated and unrelated, where an individual can apply psychological theory. You can apply psychology to many aspects of everyday life, regardless of your career or job title.

Teaching – using psychology to understand why and how students and children learn and adapting learning to different environments and audiences. This uses knowledge and applications of cognitive and neurodevelopmental psychology theories.

Management Consulting – using psychology to work with clients to improve motivation, create change initiatives or monitor organisational mergers and acquisitions. Psychological theories such as motivation and leadership theories as well as social psychology, can be applied here. Additionally, research skills such as survey design and analysis would be useful in this setting.

Project Management – project managers organise, plan, monitor and evaluate projects and make sure they are completed on time and with the correct resources. This draws upon skills learnt from a degree in psychology, including research, communication and managing modules and research studies. Additionally, social psychology theories can be applied such as social learning theory, when trying to ensure teams complete projects as well as social identity theory to create team cohesion.

These examples show that even if you don't have a psychology role that you think is related to the main applied areas of the field, you can and probably will be drawing on knowledge that you developed during your psychology degree.

WHO CAN I SPEAK TO FIND PSYCHOLOGISTS IN THE FIELD TO ASK THEM WHAT THEIR JOBS ARE LIKE?

Having access to professional psychologists may seem hard or daunting; however, there are places you can go to look and have access to professional psychologists, or to understand more deeply about what they do.

You can look at places including:

- The British Psychological Society (BPS)
- Local NHS trust
- Local councils
- University or college lecturers
- LinkedIn

These organisations and platforms are just some of the places where psychologists work, are members of or showcase themselves. Emailing psychologists or institutions is a good way to test the waters. Another way to access psychologists is to contact your university or college lecturers, as they may be connected with professional psychologists.

WHERE TO FIND PSYCHOLOGY ROLES AND WORK EXPERIENCE

Many graduates and undergraduate students struggle to find roles after their studies and may have difficulty understanding the career options available to them with a psychology degree. Table 13.2 shows possible places you can find psychology roles in for different specialisms.

With standard application forms for these roles, which you may find when applying to local government or NHS roles, or if you are used to other roles that require a CV, being clear, concise and open in your experience and why you are a suitable candidate for the job.

Table 13.2 Where to find work experience or jobs depending on the area of interest

Area of psychology	*Where to find jobs*
Forensic, clinical and counselling	NHS jobs, British Psychological Society Jobs board, Prison and Probation Service Jobs board, Papyrus, Shout, Samaritans, Women's Aid, Indeed, Total Jobs, Guardian Jobs
Educational	Local council/government jobs boards, school websites, Indeed, Total Jobs, Guardian Jobs
Sports and exercise	Gym websites, sports team's websites, Total Jobs, Guardian Jobs, Indeed
Health	Local council/government jobs boards, Total Jobs, Guardian Jobs, Indeed
Occupational/ organisational	Local council/government jobs boards, Total Jobs, Guardian Jobs, Indeed

VOLUNTARY AND PAID WORK TO DO ALONGSIDE YOUR STUDIES

Another way to gain experience is to pair voluntary work with studying and with other roles. Unfortunately, unpaid work does form a background to a psychology career, especially early on. The ethics of this are questionable; this over-reliance on voluntary roles to gain experience disproportionately affects those from lower socioeconomic backgrounds. This is due to the view that people from lower socioeconomic backgrounds cannot or may not work for free and are less likely to pursue further study.

Some people choose to pursue voluntary roles alongside paid work or while studying. In a previous chapter, we discussed undergraduate psychology programmes with placement years. These placement years allow students to experience a variety of specialisms within psychology and to gain real-world experience. As this is not available to everyone, as there aren't so many psychology degrees with this option, there are still other possibilities to help you apply some of your psychological skills to the workforce.

CHAPTER SUMMARY

- This chapter goes through frequently asked questions that someone who wants to pursue a career in psychology may ask.
- Examples of these questions include what voluntary and paid work a person can do during and after their studies, what someone can expect out of their undergraduate degree in psychology, understanding which area of psychology to pursue and what it takes to become a qualified psychologist in the UK.

14

PSYCHOLOGY IN POLICY AND SOCIAL IMPACT

Psychology, is often at the core of public policy and policy recommendations. These recommendations and full-blown policy programmes and interventions are in areas such as mental health, law, economics, social policy and employment and the roots of some of these interventions are from disciplines such as behavioural change, behavioural economics and include a lot of psychoeducation and other psychological tools to encourage healthy and socially beneficial behaviours. Here are some notable examples.

1. In the UK, the state pension changed its enrolment to an opt-out process and this shift in process raised the proportion of workers who were saving towards their retirement by a significant amount. This policy was created and developed using behavioural economics and psychology principles.
2. Another example, the UK tested communication messages to increase the number of people in the UK's organ donor register. This process was tested by the behavioural insights team, which was set up in 2010 and is part of the UK's civil service and uses insights from social psychology, behavioural economics and behavioural science to understand how people make decisions.

DOI: 10.4324/9781003669449-15

3. Another government intervention backed by psychological processes was an education policy to increase attendance and General Certificate of Secondary Education (GCSE) pass rates. The intervention started by asking young people to nominate study partners to create peer learning and motivation between students. These interventions were found to increase attendance by up to 15% and increase pass rates by 30%.[1] This intervention has psychological underpinnings.

REASONS WHY PSYCHOLOGY IS IMPORTANT IN POLICY-MAKING AND GOVERNMENT

Strong evidence base: when conducted correctly, psychological research is grounded in knowledge from primary or secondary evidence. This evidence base can take the form of laboratory studies in humans or animals, interviews, questionnaire surveys or observational studies. These pieces of evidence, although they do not provide the fullest picture of a phenomenon, offer valuable insights into how and why things might happen. This then builds an underlying picture to support theory, create or build policy.

Criminal justice and rehabilitation: forensic and academic psychologists work in these fields, observing offender behaviour and its effects on victims, families and society. Forensic and academic psychologists have a more precise view of the practical and theoretical aspects at play.

Bringing a different perspective to misinformation and bias: as psychologists are connected to research processes, as they conduct it, design it, interpret it and embed it into practice, they are in a great position to understand how to utilise research effectively. On an undergraduate psychology course, you learn about assessing and understanding research, designing credible experiments, generating both quantitative and qualitative data and understanding how to interpret and assess it. Understanding how research is done is a great underpinning to being able to weed out strong vs weak evidence.

Mental health advocacy: psychologists who specialise in mental health push for a focus and view current policies through a mental health lens. This can create support and a strong base for making mental health more important.

FUTURE OF PSYCHOLOGY CAREERS

Mental health support is increasing, with online therapy and health apps becoming more prevalent. According to Mikulic (2020),[2] in 2020, there were over 50,000 mental health apps available to download on management; however, according to Baxter et al. (2020)[3] and Lau et al. (2020),[4] only 2.08% of publicly available mobile apps have published evidence of their effectiveness.

This suggests that the whole of psychology, but especially mental health, counselling, clinical and sports and exercise psychology, has become increasingly digitised, and this has benefits; however, the introduction of digital and AI aspects isn't always positive. For example, data protection, ethics and the quality of digital interventions need to be effectively evaluated and validated.

This shows that the future of psychology careers, regardless of the applied area will have a large digital and artificial intelligence component to it. It may look a little something like this (Table 14.1).

CYBER PSYCHOLOGY

Cyber psychology examines how psychology and cyber technology intersect and how people interact with technology. It does connect with user research and user research design and research is a key component of the area of cyber psychology. Cyber psychology includes understanding how the internet, mobile phones, virtual reality, artificial intelligence, games consoles and digital media can affect human behaviour. Cyber psychology researches global trends.

If you are interested in studying cyber psychology as a module in undergraduate psychology or as a postgraduate master's degree, modules that you can cover include: principles of psychology online, psychology of gaming and multimedia entertainment, research methods, social psychology of the internet, human behaviour and cybersecurity and psychology of AI.

Table 14.1 AI and each applied area of psychology

Area of applied psychology	*AI interventions*	*Positive ethical implications*	*Negative ethical implications*
Clinical, health and counselling psychology	AI being used for note taking, analysing trends with client risk, chatbots/therapy bots, wearables	Ability to analyse trends, aid with support, more accessibility (e.g., chatbots), understand and help to create risk assessments and track risk	Data protection, possibility of algorithms not being trained on diverse populations Safety concerns with monitoring and flagging things like suicide/self-harm risk
Forensic psychology	Analysing large language models of 'offender behaviour' understand risk, provide early intervention support using possible online resources	The analysis can be used to apply to policy changes, analyse trends, early intervention programmes can be administered online to ensure they are more accessible	Data protection, bias in algorithms for gender, ethnicity etc.
Educational/developmental psychology	Note taking, assessment administration and analysis, monitoring development, understanding trends	Support with analysis of research for policy as well as programme and intervention analysis leading to recommendations, more accessibility regarding supporting SEN learners and more evidence-based AI interventions	Data protection, bias in algorithms for people from marginalised groups

(*Continued*)

Table 14.1 (Continued)

Area of applied psychology	*AI interventions*	*Positive ethical implications*	*Negative ethical implications*
Occupational psychology	Psychometric analysis and administration for selection and assessment and coaching Understanding employee data such as wellbeing, job satisfaction, intentions to leave, analysing work meetings, research analysis	Can help with analysing data, coming up with big trend analysis of themes within workplace settings Online coaching and mentoring interventions aided by AI Applicant tracking systems for recruitment	Data protection and ethnical implications, ensuring biases aren't involved within the AI systems and ensure things are put in place to circumvent this
Sports and exercise psychology	Understanding performance prediction and talent identification across different sports AI in gamification of goal setting and visualisation Performance analysis	Sports medicine, injury diagnosis etc., wearable tech in exercise and performance metrics and gamifications	Data protection and ethnical implications, ensuring biases aren't involved within the AI systems and ensure things are put in place to circumvent this

RESEARCH IN CYBER PSYCHOLOGY

Different research topics in the area can include things like

- E-commerce and online shopping
- Mobile device behaviour
- Virtual communities and blogging behaviour
- Social networking
- Augmented reality
- Addiction and cyberporn

"From Setback to Come Back: A Virtual Reality Based Self-Compassion Intervention for Injured Athletes," "Does Digital Intergroup Contact Reduce Prejudice? A Meta-Analysis," and "Can Media Literacy Intervention Improve Fake News Credibility Assessment? A Meta-Analysis." These are three research papers currently in the Journal of *Cyberpsychology, Behaviour and Social Networking.*

CAREERS IN CYBER PSYCHOLOGY

- You can do a PhD research programme and become a researcher or an academic psychologist focussed on cyber psychology.
- You can work in organisations that focus on developing digital products and services such as social and digital media organisations.
- You can also work in user research roles in a variety of organisations, as well as working in virtual reality companies.
- Cybersecurity is another viable job area for cyber psychologists.

PSYCHOLOGY CAREERS AND AI

Although no one can predict the future, the impact of artificial intelligence on psychology careers may be great. Psychologists are increasingly reported to use AI tools to streamline their practice; according to the American Psychological Association and a 2024 practitioner survey, one in ten use AI at least monthly for notetaking and administration.[5]

AI tools can be used in research to code qualitative research and be used to support idea generation in research, lesson plans in the teaching of psychology and there are many more uses such as the use of chatbots for counselling and clinical psychology to reduce symptoms of anxiety and depression.

We can predict that artificial intelligence will be used more widely and will affect the psychology profession. Based on this, there are serious ethical and psychological conditions that we need to be aware of and consider.

According to a British Psychological Society article by Ian MacRae (2004),[6] if using AI to outline key topics, conduct literature reviews, or analyse data, ensure you use a verifiable set of sources and that the information is checked by those who can assess its accuracy. There are specialist research artificial intelligence chatbots that are likely to be more accurate than general AI tools.

Another area of caution is to avoid sharing confidential or private data, such as personal information, because there is no way to know how it will be shared. This use may breach general data protection regulation (GDPR) guidelines.

Another point is that people should be careful about using text that is generated by generative AI, so you can attribute the source information accurately. Additionally, there are many objections to the use of AI on ethical and environmental grounds.

CHAPTER SUMMARY

In summary, psychology careers are vast and diverse. Studying the subject at degree level opens up a range of careers, including applied psychology (e.g., clinical, counselling, or forensic psychology) and areas such as user research or human resources.

Even though popular belief sometimes highlights psychology as a 'Mickey Mouse' degree, something that is not a serious area of specialism or worth studying, this whole book highlights how useful psychology is to everyday life. Psychology degrees don't just expand your knowledge in so many areas; they also allow you to learn about yourself and be self-aware.

The main takeaways from this book are that you need to:

1. Research the area/s of psychology you are interested in.
2. Research how you want to study: through a BA or BSc degree, part-time or full-time, with a placement year or without?
3. Gain some kind of work experience in those areas, along with reading and engaging with your studies. You can do this by interacting with lecturers and teachers, networking with classmates and seeking both informal and formal work.
4. After your undergraduate degree, if you want to pursue further study, research which master's or professional doctorates you are interested in and the work experience you will need.
5. If you don't want to complete a doctorate, you can research various other similar roles and associates' professions that align with psychology.
6. If you want to do another non-related role outside of psychology and still use your degree, there are several professions that lend themselves well to psychology.

Whatever you want to do with your psychology knowledge and skills, studying the subject is never a waste of time.

NOTES

1 https://educationendowmentfoundation.org.uk/education-evidence/teaching-learning-toolkit/peer-tutoring
2 Mikulic, M. (2020). *Number of mHealth Apps available in the App store from 1st quarter 2015 to 1st quarter 2020.* Statista
3 Baxter, C., Carroll, J. A., Keogh, B., & Vandelanotte, C. (2020). Assessment of mobile health apps using built in smartphone sensors for diagnosis and treatment: Systematic survey of apps listed in international curated health app libraries. *JMIR Mhealth Uhealth*, 8(2), 16741.
4 Lau, N., O'Daffer, A., Colt, S., Joyce, P., Palermo, T. M., McCauley, E., & Rosenberg, A. T. (2020). Android and iphone mobile apps for psychosocial wellness and stress management: Systematic

search in app stores and literature review. *JMIR Mhealth Uhealth*, 8(5), 17798.

5 *Barriers to care in a changing practice environment: 2024 practitioner pulse survey*, Dec 2024. American Psychological Association. https://www.apa.org/pubs/reports/practitioner/2024/practitioner-pulse-2024-full-report.pdf

6 MacRae, I. (2024). AI and the work of psychologists: Practical applications and ethical considerations. bps.org.uk.

GLOSSARY OF KEY TERMS

Accreditation – A formal recognition that a course or qualification meets the standards set by a professional body, for psychology in the UK that is the British Psychological Society.

Applied Psychology – The practical use of psychological theories, methods and research to solve real-world problems and this represents areas including forensic, counselling, clinical, occupational, sports and exercise, health and educational psychology as well as areas like neuropsychology and cyber psychology.

Assistant Psychologist – Work in variety of roles and support people with mental health conditions. Assistant psychologists work as part of a multidisciplinary team, and you'll provide support to patients, and you will be supervised by a qualified psychologist.

Assessment – The systematic process of gathering information to understand psychological functioning, needs, or difficulties.

BPS (British Psychological Society) – The professional body for psychologists in the UK responsible for accreditation of courses, standards and professional development.

Burnout – A state of emotional, physical and mental exhaustion caused by prolonged stress, commonly referenced in caring and helping professions.

CASES – Chartered Association of Sport and Exercise Sciences. For Sports and Exercise Psychologists, they may want to obtain an additional accreditation with this professional body.

Chartered Psychologist – A psychologist who has met the BPS's standards for education, training, and supervised practice. Chartered psychologists need to have completed a professional doctorate such as the DClin Psych qualification or have done an equivalent chartered psychology route for each area of applied psychology. The non-professional doctorate route allows a person, after their master's degree to complete supervised practice whilst working and can be completed in sports and exercise, health, occupational, forensic and counselling psychology.

Clinical Psychology – A branch of psychology focused on the assessment and treatment of mental health difficulties across the lifespan.

Competency Framework – A structured outline of skills, knowledge and behaviours required for effective professional practice.

Conversion Course – A postgraduate psychology degree that allows graduates from other disciplines to gain BPS-accredited status. For example, if someone has completed a degree in another subject and wants to become a chartered psychologist, they may need to complete a Psychology conversion course, which takes up to two years part-time or one year full-time.

Counselling Psychology – A psychology specialism integrating therapeutic practice with psychological theory, often emphasising relational and reflective work.

Doctorate – An advanced qualification completed after undergraduate degrees (e.g. DClinPsy, DEdPsy, PhD) is required for qualification in most applied psychology roles. Doctoral qualifications include professional doctorates like DEdPsy or DClinPsy as well as PhDs. PhDs are research doctorates and professional doctorates have practical elements including placements as well as research elements.

Educational Psychology – A branch of psychology concerned with learning, development and wellbeing in educational contexts.

Evidence-Based Practice – The integration of research evidence in psychological work.

Forensic Psychology – The application of psychology within legal and criminal justice settings.

Formulation – A collaborative psychological explanation of a person's difficulties that links theory to lived experience.

Graduate Basis for Chartered Membership (GBC) – The foundational status required to progress into postgraduate psychology training in the UK. The GBC confirms you have studied psychology at a particular level and depth equivalent to a second-class psychology undergraduate degree. If you have studied another subject and want to convert to psychology, doing a psychology conversion master's will help you switch.

HCPC (Health and Care Professions Council) – The statutory regulator for practitioner psychologists and other health professionals in the UK.

Health Psychology – A field of psychology examining how biological, psychological and social factors influence health and illness.

Imposter Syndrome – Persistent self-doubt and fear of being exposed as inadequate despite evidence of competence.

Inclusion – Practices that ensure people from diverse backgrounds feel valued, represented and able to progress.

Interdisciplinary Working – Collaboration across professional boundaries (e.g. psychology, social work, medicine).

Master's Degree – A postgraduate qualification (level 7 in the UK) that signifies advanced, specialist knowledge in an area. Masters are characterised into a Master of Arts (MA) and Master of Science (MSc). There are also MRes (Master of Research) or MPhil (Master of Philosophy).

Mentorship – Developmental support provided by a more experienced professional to guide career progression.

NHS/National Health Service – The UK's NHS/ National Health Service is funded by the UK taxpayer and offers physical and mental health services to those in need, free at the point of service.

Neuropsychology – A specialist field exploring the relationship between brain function and behaviour. In the UK

Neuropsychology is a route for clinical psychologists once they have qualified.

Occupational Psychology – The application of psychology to work, organisations, and employee wellbeing.

Placement – A period of supervised practical experience completed as part of training or preparation for professional roles.

Professional Identity – A person's sense of themselves as a practitioner, shaped by values, training and experience.

Psychological Wellbeing – A broad concept encompassing mental health, emotional resilience and life satisfaction.

Psychologist – A protected title referring to professionals who have completed accredited training and are registered with a regulatory body.

Psychometrics – The science of psychological measurement, including tests of ability, personality and wellbeing.

Reflective Practice – The ongoing process of critically examining one's work, values, and impact to improve professional effectiveness. This is common in all the applied areas of psychology and research.

Research Literacy – The ability to understand, evaluate and apply psychological research.

Self-Care – Strategies used by individuals to maintain well-being and prevent burnout in demanding roles.

SEPAR – Sport and Exercise Accreditation Route is organised by CASES (Chartered Association of Sport and Exercise Sciences), and this can be an additional or alternative route for sports and exercise psychologists to register with the Health Care Professions Council (HCPC).

Specialism – A focused area of psychological practice requiring additional training (e.g. clinical, forensic, educational).

Supervision – A structured professional relationship providing support, awareness, oversight, and development.

Transferable Skills – Skills gained through psychology training (e.g. analysis, communication) that apply across different careers.

Values-Based Career Choice – Selecting career paths aligned with personal values, ethics, and meaning.

REFERENCES

Arthur, M., Claman, P., & DeFillippi, R. (1995). Intelligent enterprise, intelligent careers. *Academy of Management Executive*, 9(4), 7–19.

Bandura, A. (1986). *Social foundations of thought and action: A social cognitive theory*. Prentice Hall.

Barriers to care in a changing practice environment: 2024 practitioner pulse survey, Dec 2024. American Psychological Association.

Baxter, C., Carroll, J. A., Keogh, B., & Vandelanotte, C. (2020). Assessment of mobile health apps using built in smartphone sensors for diagnosis and treatment: Systematic survey of apps listed in international curated health app libraries. *JMIR Mhealth Uhealth*, 8(2), 16741.

Health and Care Professionals Council (2020). Diversity data report 2021. https://www.hcpc-uk.org/resources/reports/2021/diversity-data-report-2021/

HESA (2022). Higher Education Student Statistics: UK, 2020/21 – Where students come from and go to study. https://www.hesa.

ac.uk/news/25-01-2022/sb262-higher-education-student-statistics/location

Holland, J. L. (1997). *Making vocational choices. A theory of vocational personalities and work environments* (3rd ed.). Psychological Assessment Resources.

https://quarterly.blog.gov.uk/2019/10/30/finding-the-unicorns-behavioural-science-in-government-grows-up

https://www.britannica.com/science/applied-psychology

https://www.gov.uk/student-finance/who-qualifies

https://www.hee.nhs.uk/our-work/mental-health/psychological-professions/improving-equity-inclusion-people-access-psychological-professions-training

https://www.ucas.com/money-and-student-life/money/scholarships-grants-and-bursaries

Hunt, A. N., & Rhodes, T. D. (2021). Expanding the life-span, life-space approach using critical race theory and intersectionality. *Journal of College Access*, 6(3), Article 8.

Kancelijak, D., & Calia, C. (2023). Section 1: Human rights and professional engagement. Diversity and inclusion in UK psychology: A nationwide survey. *Clinical Psychology Forum*, 369, 25–29.

Lau, N., O'Daffer, A., Colt, S., Joyce, P., Palermo, T. M., McCauley, E., & Rosenberg, A. T. (2020). Android and iphone mobile apps for psychosocial wellness and stress management: Systematic search in app stores and literature review. *JMIR Mhealth Uhealth*, 8(5), 17798.

Lent, R. W., & Brown, S. D. (2013). *Career self-management: A social cognitive perspective.* In S. D. Brown & R. W. Lent (Eds.), *Career development and counseling: Putting theory and research to work* (2nd ed., pp. 381–411). Wiley.

Lent, R. W., Brown, S. D., & Hackett, G. (1994). Toward a unifying social cognitive theory of career and academic interest, choice, and performance. *Journal of Vocational Behavior*, 45(1), 79–122.

MacRae, I. (2024). AI and the work of psychologists: Practical applications and ethical considerations. bps.org.uk.

Mainiero, L. A., & Sullivan, S. E. (2005). Kaleidoscope careers: An alternate explanation for the opt-out revolution. *The Academy of Management Executive*, 19(1), 106–123.

Mikulic, M. (2020). *Number of mHealth Apps available in the App store from 1st quarter 2015 to 1st quarter 2020*. Statista.

Super, D. E. (1953). A theory of vocational development. *American Psychologist*, 8(5), 185–190.

UNESCO Institute of Statistics (2021). Education – Outbound internationally mobile students by host region. Available at https://data.uis.unesco.org/

UUKi (2021). Why aren't we second? Pt.2. Available at International student recruitment: Why aren't we second? Part 2 (universitiesuk.ac.uk).

Warr, P. (Ed.). (2002). *Psychology at work* (5th ed., pp. 182–183). Penguin Press.

What Do Graduates Do? 2024/2025 Produced by Prospects (Part of Jisc) and AGCAS. https://graduatemarkettrends.cdn.prismic.io/graduatemarkettrends/aQ4HjLpReVYa4PSy_what-do-graduates-do-2024.pdf

INDEX

Note: **Bold** page numbers refer to tables and *italic* page numbers refer to figures.

For Product Safety Concerns and Information please contact our EU representative GPSR@taylorandfrancis.com Taylor & Francis Verlag GmbH, Kaufingerstraße 24, 80331 München, Germany